OCT'1 4

Can Gun Control Reduce Violence?

Patricia D. Netzley

INCONTROVERSY

ReferencePoint Press®

San Diego, CA

© 2014 ReferencePoint Press, Inc.
Printed in the United States

For more information, contact:
ReferencePoint Press, Inc.
PO Box 27779
San Diego, CA 92198
www. ReferencePointPress.com

LIBRARY OF CONGRESS CATALOGING-IN-PUBLICATION DATA

Netzley, Patricia D.
   Can gun control reduce violence? / by Patricia D. Netzley.
     pages cm. -- (In controversy)
   Includes bibliographical references and index.
   Audience: Grade 9 to 12.
   ISBN-13: 978-1-60152-604-5 (hardback)
   ISBN-10: 1-60152-604-0 (hardback)
 1. Gun control--United States. 2. Violent crimes--United States. 3. Firearms--United States.
 4. Firearms--Law and legislation--United States. 5. Violent crimes--United States--Prevention. I. Title.
   HV7436.N48   2014
   363.330973--dc23
                                                             2013019892

Contents

Foreword

In 2008, as the US economy and economies worldwide were falling into the worst recession since the Great Depression, most Americans had difficulty comprehending the complexity, magnitude, and scope of what was happening. As is often the case with a complex, controversial issue such as this historic global economic recession, looking at the problem as a whole can be overwhelming and often does not lead to understanding. One way to better comprehend such a large issue or event is to break it into smaller parts. The intricacies of global economic recession may be difficult to understand, but one can gain insight by instead beginning with an individual contributing factor, such as the real estate market. When examined through a narrower lens, complex issues become clearer and easier to evaluate.

This is the idea behind ReferencePoint Press's *In Controversy* series. The series examines the complex, controversial issues of the day by breaking them into smaller pieces. Rather than looking at the stem cell research debate as a whole, a title would examine an important aspect of the debate such as *Is Stem Cell Research Necessary?* or *Is Embryonic Stem Cell Research Ethical?* By studying the central issues of the debate individually, researchers gain a more solid and focused understanding of the topic as a whole.

Each book in the series provides a clear, insightful discussion of the issues, integrating facts and a variety of contrasting opinions for a solid, balanced perspective. Personal accounts and direct quotes from academic and professional experts, advocacy groups, politicians, and others enhance the narrative. Sidebars add depth to the discussion by expanding on important ideas and events. For quick reference, a list of key facts concludes every chapter. Source notes, an annotated organizations list, bibliography, and index provide student researchers with additional tools for papers and class discussion.

The *In Controversy* series also challenges students to think critically about issues, to improve their problem-solving skills, and to sharpen their ability to form educated opinions. As President Barack Obama stated in a March 2009 speech, success in the twenty-first century will not be measurable merely by students' ability to "fill in a bubble on a test but whether they possess 21st century skills like problem-solving and critical thinking and entrepreneurship and creativity." Those who possess these skills will have a strong foundation for whatever lies ahead.

No one can know for certain what sort of world awaits today's students. What we can assume, however, is that those who are inquisitive about a wide range of issues; open-minded to divergent views; aware of bias and opinion; and able to reason, reflect, and reconsider will be best prepared for the future. As the international development organization Oxfam notes, "Today's young people will grow up to be the citizens of the future: but what that future holds for them is uncertain. We can be quite confident, however, that they will be faced with decisions about a wide range of issues on which people have differing, contradictory views. If they are to develop as global citizens all young people should have the opportunity to engage with these controversial issues."

In Controversy helps today's students better prepare for tomorrow. An understanding of the complex issues that drive our world and the ability to think critically about them are essential components of contributing, competing, and succeeding in the twenty-first century.

Protection or Threat?

In March 2013 a committee of Colorado state senators held a hearing to allow people to express their opinions on seven proposed gun control laws, including a bill that would ban the carrying of concealed weapons on college campuses. Those who testified in favor of this ban argued that guns were unnecessary and perhaps dangerous to have at school. For example, one student stated, "A learning environment is no place for weaponry. The classroom is not a warzone, a firing range, a hunting ground. . . . There is no need for firearms in a controlled environment such as school." Another student said, "I do not want to carry a weapon. I should not have to carry a weapon in order to feel safe." A teacher insisted, "I feel better when the [campus] police have guns and my angry student doesn't."[1]

However, those on the other side of the issue insisted that they would feel less safe if the ban was enacted. For example, Adam Thompson, who was a junior at Colorado's Columbine High School in 1999 when two of his classmates killed thirteen people in a shooting spree he barely escaped, said, "I was put in a position where I was defenseless and so were the people around me that were supposed to keep me safe. I never want to be defenseless again. . . . I have become a firearms owner."[2]

A Feeling of Defenselessness

The most outspoken opponent of the ban was rape survivor Amanda Collins. She was attacked in 2007 in a parking lot just

"I feel better when the [campus] police have guns and my angry student doesn't."[1]

— A teacher at a 2013 gun control law debate in Colorado.

50 feet (15 m) from the campus police office at the University of Nevada–Reno. But because it happened late at night, the office was closed, the police had gone home, and there was no one else around to hear her cries for help. Moreover, although Collins had a second-degree black belt in taekwondo at the time, her martial arts skills were an inadequate defense against her bigger, stronger attacker, later identified as serial rapist James Biela.

Collins therefore argued that the only way she could have fended off Biela was with a gun. She told the committee that she had a permit to carry a concealed weapon but had not been armed on the night of her attack because her university did not allow students to carry guns. She was sure that had she been allowed access to her firearm, she could have shot and killed Biela, even though he had a gun as well. "I know without a doubt in my mind, at some point, I would have been able to stop my attack by using my firearm,"[3] she insisted.

Moreover, because Biela went on to rape two more women and murder another after attacking Collins, she stated, "If I had been carrying that night, two other rapes would have been prevented and a young life would have been saved."[4] One of the senators at the hearing, Evie Hudak, disagreed. Hudak told the young woman, "You said that you were a martial arts student . . . experienced in taekwondo. And yet because this individual was so large, was able to overcome you even with your skills, chances are that if you had had a gun, he would have been able to get that from you and possibly use it against you."[5]

Collins countered that Biela already had his own weapon and therefore would not have needed to take hers. Nonetheless, Hudak remained firm in her belief that Collins would have been putting her life at greater risk by pulling out a gun. To support her position, Hudak cited a statistic from the Colorado Coalition Against Gun Violence indicating that "for every one woman who used a handgun to kill someone in self-defense, 83 were murdered by them."[6]

The next day many people criticized the senator for the harsh way in which she had responded to Collins's painful experience. Hudak apologized for this before explaining why she had abruptly brought up statistics. "Amid this emotional testimony," she said, "my goal was to share research data about the increased danger of having a gun in an assault."[7]

Controversial Statistics

However, no studies have been done on how many women have been murdered by a man using the woman's own gun against her. In fact, reliable data on many aspects of gun use is hard to come by. Because the issue of gun control is so polarizing, some researchers have avoided studying subjects related to gun violence altogether. Others have come up with widely different results depending on where and when they conducted their studies, how study participants were chosen, and many other factors.

For example, criminologist Gary Kleck conducted a survey that found there are more than 2 million instances a year of people using a gun to defend themselves. However, his definition of "defensive gun use" includes cases where someone pulls out a gun upon hearing a frightening noise in the backyard only to find out that no one is there. Studies with a narrower definition of "defensive gun use" have come up with a range of 370,000 to 100,000 instances or fewer. Given these disparities, James Q. Wilson, a public policy expert at the University of California–Los Angeles, says: "We don't know what the right number is." But he also notes that since none of the figures is small, "whatever the right number is, it's not a trivial number."[8]

There are, however, some reliable statistics available on how many people are killed by guns each year. According to the Centers for Disease Control and Prevention, in 2005—the most recent year for which the government offers complete data on the number of reported firearm fatalities in the United States—gun use resulted in the deaths of 30,143 Americans. Of these, 12,352 were homicides, 17,002 were suicides, and 789 were accidental deaths. In addition, nearly 70,000 people suffered a gun-related injury that was not fatal.

Unknown is how often a person points a gun at someone who turns out to be harmless. Nonetheless, some think that the risk of mistaking a harmless person for a dangerous one is high. For example, in commenting on Collins's pro-gun arguments, Colo-

rado representative Joe Salazar says that young women "couldn't possibly know if they are in danger. And you don't know if you feel like you're gonna be raped, or if you feel like someone's been following you around or if you feel like you're in trouble when you may actually not be, that you pop out that gun and you pop . . . pop around at somebody."[9] Collins counters, "So, is he saying that all women are unable to make sound decisions in the midst of that, that we should go against our God given gut instinct that something was wrong? I knew something was wrong the moment I was grabbed from behind."[10]

Collins also criticizes a suggestion made by Salazar and others that a rape whistle would be an adequate defense for women afraid of being attacked, since in her case there was no one around to hear a whistle. Moreover, she believes that no one should be able to decide for her what she should use in her own defense. She states, "My choice in how I want to protect myself should not be mandated by the government."[11]

Law enforcement authorities collected hundreds of guns (pictured) in a 2013 New Jersey buyback program that offered cash for guns. Guns kill thousands of people in the United States each year and some communities have turned to buyback programs to reduce the number of guns.

Limiting Access

Proponents of tougher gun control laws argue that a person's choice of weaponry should be limited because that choice can impact other people. Having a gun handy, they say, makes it easier for one person to shoot another while drunk, angry, or upset, even when the target is a friend or relative. Drawing on several studies, Marty Langley, policy analyst for the Violence Policy Center, reports, "In 2010, 94 percent of the women killed by men were done so by someone they knew. Of that figure, 64 percent were wives, ex-wives or girlfriends."[12] In other words, most victims of gun violence know the shooter personally.

Guns are also a major factor in suicide. According to the US Bureau of Justice Statistics, among people over age twenty, 60 percent of gun deaths are suicides, whereas only 37 percent are homicides. Consequently, Augustine J. Kposowa, a sociology professor at the University of California–Riverside, says, "Research shows that when a gun is used in the home, it is often against household members in the commission of homicides or suicides."[13]

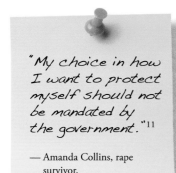

"My choice in how I want to protect myself should not be mandated by the government."[11]

— Amanda Collins, rape survivor.

In addition, a gun owned by a law-abiding citizen can be stolen by a criminal who might then use it in violent crimes. According to the US Department of Justice, from 2005 through 2010 about 1.4 million guns were stolen during household burglaries and other property crimes. About four out of five of these firearms, most of them handguns, were never recovered. But Collins rejects the notion that her carrying of a gun has anything to do with crime rates, saying, "How does rendering me defenseless protect you against a violent crime?"[14]

After the hearing, she received a great deal of media attention for her opposition to the campus gun ban, and senators' support for the bill dropped so low that the measure was never even voted on. This lack of political support is common when it comes to legislation on gun control. Kposowa reports, "Even modest efforts to reform gun laws are typically met with vehement opposition."[15] This is true even after a particularly heinous act of gun violence is committed, such as a school shooting that kills innocent children. Sometimes new laws are passed as a result of these tragedies, but in many cases their scope is limited. Moreover, even when tough gun control laws are passed—as in Colorado after the 2012 movie theater shooting—such laws are often called into question because of disagreement over the effectiveness of reducing gun violence through legislation. In fact, people cannot even agree on the root causes of gun violence. Consequently, gun control remains one of the most controversial issues in America today.

Facts

- **Gun violence experts and the National Rifle Association (NRA) generally agree that there are more than 300 million guns in the United States, a statistic based on firearm production data, gun sales figures, and gun owner surveys.**

- **In 2010 the FBI received more than eight thousand reports of criminals using a gun to commit a homicide.**

- **In 2010, of the 230 cases reported to the FBI of a justifiable homicide committed by a private citizen using a firearm, more than a third featured a victim who was known to the shooter.**

What Are the Origins of the Gun Control Controversy?

O n the morning of January 17, 1989, a twenty-four-year-old man named Patrick Edward Purdy drove to an area behind his former grammar school, Cleveland Elementary, in Stockton, California. He was wearing a flak jacket, which would protect him from bullet wounds if anyone shot at him, and carried a semi-automatic assault rifle as well as a pistol. He had also plugged up his ears so that his hearing would not be harmed by loud gunfire.

Once out of his car, he used a gasoline-filled bottle to set his vehicle on fire, and because the car contained fireworks, it exploded. By now the time was nearly noon, and the schoolyard was filled with roughly three hundred children in grades K through 3. Purdy walked to the yard and opened fire on the children. Within three minutes he had fired 106 rounds as children and teachers screamed and ran. "He was just standing there with a gun, making wide sweeps," Lori Mackey, then a teacher at the school, subsequently told a reporter. "He was not talking, he was not yelling, he was very straight-faced. It did not look like he was really angry; it was just matter-of-factly. . . . There was mass chaos. There were kids running in every direction."[16]

Purdy shot thirty-four children and one teacher, and five of

12

the children died. Then he used his pistol to shoot and kill himself. The resulting scene was horrific. Arson investigator Marty Galindo, who was called to the school because of the car fire and explosion, later said, "I can still smell the gunpowder. That's what I remember most—the gunpowder. There were bullet casings everywhere. . . . I walked around the corner of a building and saw all those kids down. It was surreal. This was supposed to be where kids are playing games, happy."[17]

Four of the students Purdy killed, all six to nine years old, were the children of Cambodian refugees who had left their homeland because of genocide. The fifth was the child of Vietnamese parents who had fled their country because of the Vietnam War. Consequently, in the aftermath of the massacre, most people assumed that Purdy's motivation was racism. However, people who knew the man said that Purdy was angry at everyone, not just Asians, and no evidence of his having specific anti-Asian views was ever found.

Then the media began reporting that Purdy had a history of mental illness, and many assumed this was the reason for his actions. However, he left behind no writings that might indicate his mental problems were the reason he decided to massacre schoolchildren. The chief investigator in the case, Captain Dennis Perry, therefore noted, "He did not leave us a message. Without that we'll never know exactly why he did what he did."[18]

Outrage over Access to Assault Weapons

What is known, however, is that Purdy had a long history of petty arrests, and many people believe this should have prevented him from owning a gun. His crimes included possessing an illegal weapon, most likely with an intent to sell it, helping someone commit an armed robbery, and shooting a semiautomatic gun at trees in a national forest. However, he spent very little time in jail for these offenses, and even though he tried to commit suicide twice while in custody, he was soon back out on the street. An alcoholic and a drug addict, he lived as a drifter.

Because Purdy had never been legally declared mentally ill and was never convicted of a crime that would have made it illegal for him to buy a gun, he had no trouble getting the weapon he used in the massacre. Nonetheless, a *Time* magazine editorial published shortly after the killings said, "Why could Purdy, an alcoholic who had been arrested for such offenses as selling weapons and attempted robbery, walk into a gun shop in Sandy, Oregon, and leave with an AK-47 [assault rifle] under his arm? The easy availability of weapons like this, which have no purpose other than killing human beings, can all too readily turn the delusions of sick gunmen into tragic nightmares."[19]

The *Time* editorial was mistaken in referring to Purdy's automatic weapon as an AK-47, a specific type of military assault rifle. However, many other media reports made the same mistake, since the gun Purdy used was extremely similar to an AK-47. Consequently, many people channeled their anger over the killings into a demand that the government ban the ownership of AK-47s. This led to discussions about types of assault weapons, and arguments ensued over how to define such guns and which ones should be banned.

The National Rifle Association (NRA), a powerful lobby for gun owners and manufacturers, spoke out against any kind of assault weapons ban. The group argued that it was too difficult to distinguish between assault weapons and ordinary rifles, and it insisted that a ban would be worthless because criminals would still be able to get such guns illegally. Nonetheless, California legislators were able to pass the first assault weapons ban in the nation.

Called the Roberti-Roos Assault Weapons Control Act of 1989, this legislation banned more than fifty makes and models of rifles, pistols, and shotguns, all semiautomatic firearms that the law specifically classified as assault weapons. In addition, the law banned any gun magazine from holding more than ten rounds of ammunition. Any weapons similar to those banned but not mentioned specifically by name were still allowed, as were any guns already owned by people at the time the law was passed. In this way, legislators were able to exclude models of guns popular with hunters and to avoid the prospect of having to take guns away from their owners. Many people consider the passage of the act

> "The easy availability of weapons like this, which have no purpose other than killing human beings, can all too readily turn the delusions of sick gunmen into tragic nightmares."[19]
>
> — A January 30, 1989, *Time* magazine editorial on the Stockton, California, school shooting.

to be the start of the modern gun control controversy, because the arguments surrounding it are similar to those associated with proposed or enacted gun control laws today.

Judging the Constitutionality of Gun Bans

Immediately after the passage of the Roberti-Roos Act, legal challenges to the law's constitutionality began. Gun rights advocates insist the Second Amendment to the US Constitution protects the right to keep and bear arms. The amendment states, "A well regulated militia, being necessary to the security of a free state, the right of the people to keep and bear arms, shall not be infringed."[20]

This wording has been interpreted in various ways, particularly in regard to the definition of *militia*. Historians note that at the time the Constitution was written, militias were military forces made up of all-white, able-bodied male citizens who were expected to provide their own guns if called upon to protect America. These militias were under the control of the states, but the US government had the right to federalize them as needed to defend the country.

Moreover, the Militia Acts of 1792, two statutes enacted by Congress that year, actually mandated that all white men between ages eighteen and forty-five have their own muskets, bayonets, bullets (specifically, twenty-four per man), and other military supplies necessary to serve effectively in state militias. Men who had their own rifles in addition to muskets also had to supply their own gunpowder and rifle balls. In addition, every militia member had to report for mandatory training twice a year. This training served the country well on several occasions, when militias were used to put down rebellions. For example, President George Washington called on a militia in 1794 to put down a rebellion in western Pennsylvania, and during the War of 1812 militias were a vital defense against the invading British.

> "A well regulated militia, being necessary to the security of a free state, the right of the people to keep and bear arms, shall not be infringed."[20]
>
> — The Second Amendment to the US Constitution.

The War of 1812 also showed that many people were willing to volunteer to fight in such causes as opposed to being mandated to fight in them. Consequently, several states abandoned mandatory

The Second Amendment to the US Constitution lies at the heart of the debate over which limits, if any, should be placed on gun ownership in America. The concise twenty-seven word amendment has been interpreted in many different ways.

militia enrollment in favor of establishing volunteer armies. This meant that fewer men needed to own guns, especially since by this time the federal government had decided to maintain a standing regular army that would be at the ready even in times of peace. After the Spanish-American War of 1898, the size of this army was greatly expanded. Nonetheless, many American men continued to own firearms, believing that no man should be without a gun.

Early Gun Control

On America's frontier in the nineteenth century, a gun could indeed be a necessity. However, frontier towns also had so much trouble with gun violence during this period that some of them banned guns in specific places. For example, in Tombstone, Arizona, it was illegal to carry a concealed firearm within the town limits, and in 1880 this ban was extended to include guns carried openly as well. Law professor Adam Winkler, author of the book *Gunfight: The Battle over the Right to Bear Arms in America*, reports:

> Out in the untamed wilderness, you needed a gun to be safe from bandits, natives, and wildlife. In the cities and towns of the West, however, the law often prohibited people from toting their guns around. A visitor arriving in Wichita, Kansas in 1873, the heart of the Wild West era, would have seen signs declaring, "Leave Your Revolvers At Police Headquarters, and Get a Check."

> A check? That's right. When you entered a frontier town, you were legally required to leave your guns at the stables on the outskirts of town or drop them off with the sheriff, who would give you a token in exchange. You checked your guns then like you'd check your overcoat today at a Boston restaurant in winter. Visitors were welcome, but their guns were not.[21]

When Georgia became the first state to ban guns, however, the constitutionality of its law was challenged. Passed in 1837, Georgia's law prohibited the sale and concealed carrying of knives used for offensive or defensive purposes, as well as the open or concealed carrying of all pistols except horse pistols, which were a type of gun carried in a holster at the front of a saddle for protection while riding. The law was in effect for eight years before the state supreme court ruled, in response to an appeal by a man who had been arrested and convicted for openly carrying a pistol, that the ban could not stand. In making its ruling, the court looked to the US Constitution, because Georgia's state constitution included no right to bear arms, and declared that while states could deny someone the right to carry a weapon in secret, no state could deny a citizen the federally protected right to openly keep a gun for defensive purposes.

"Visitors were welcome, but their guns were not."[21]

— Adam Winkler, gun history expert, on frontier towns in the late nineteenth century.

During the nineteenth century, however, people increasingly thought of defense as more the responsibility of the government than of individual citizens. This perception was aided in part by laws that strengthened police and military forces. For example, in 1903 the Dick Act affirmed the National Guard, rather than citizen militias, as the reserve force of the United States. In addition, states enacted laws that restricted the ways in which individuals could use guns. For example, in 1911 New York passed the Sullivan Act, which required that guns small enough to be concealed while carried had to be licensed with the state.

The Sullivan Act was a response to a shocking murder-suicide that took place in January 1911 in New York City. The victim was a well-known journalist, David Graham Phillips, who had written a novel that attracted the attention of a mentally unstable violinist, Fitzhugh Coyle Goldsborough. Goldsborough believed that Phillips had used Goldsborough's sister as a model for a character in the book who was portrayed in an unseemly way. Consequently,

Guns were a necessity on the American frontier in the 1800s. They were used for hunting and for protection, but to avoid unnecessary violence some towns required visitors to check their guns during their stay.

he confronted Phillips on the street and shot him six times before shooting himself in the head. Goldsborough died instantly, but Phillips did not die until the following evening. Almost immediately thereafter, someone working in the coroner's office, George Petit le Brun, started a letter-writing campaign that convinced politicians to act. "I reasoned that the time had come to prevent the sale of pistols to irresponsible persons,"[22] he later said.

The National Firearms Act

Another gun control law that resulted from a crime-inspired public outcry came into being after the Saint Valentine's Day Massacre of 1929. In this incident five members of a Chicago criminal outfit and two collaborators were lined up along a wall inside a city garage, sprayed with gunfire from submachine guns, and then blasted with shotguns by a rival gang. In the aftermath of the massacre—a time when gangster violence was a growing problem in the United States—the government worked to pass a law that would regulate weapons commonly used by gangsters. These included machine guns (which are fully automatic firearms designed to keep firing as long as the trigger is depressed) and short-barreled shotguns.

The ultimate result of this work was the National Firearms Act of 1934, which taxed certain kinds of firearms and required those firearms to be registered with a unit of the Bureau of Internal Revenue (now the Internal Revenue Service). In 1938 the law was challenged as unconstitutional by Paul E. Gutensohn, the defense attorney in a case against bank robbers Jack Miller and Frank Layton. These men had been caught with an unregistered short-barreled shotgun, and Gutensohn argued that the Second Amendment, by protecting state militias, protected gun owners from interference by the federal government.

The resulting legal case, *United States v. Miller*, eventually found its way to the US Supreme Court, and in 1939 the justices ruled that the law was constitutional. In its ruling, the court stated:

> In the absence of any evidence tending to show that possession or use of a "shotgun having a barrel of less than eighteen inches in length" at this time has some reasonable

Mandatory Gun Ownership

All of America's original thirteen colonies except Pennsylvania (founded by Quaker pacifists) mandated gun possession to varying degrees. Some even had laws requiring men to bring their guns to worship meetings because of threats of attack by Native Americans. Given this historical precedent, modern lawmakers have suggested mandating gun ownership as well. In 1982, for example, Kennesaw, Georgia passed an ordinance requiring households to have at least one firearm and its ammunition. This action was an expression of support for gun rights following the passage of a gun ban in Morton Grove, Illinois. But in March 2013 the town of Nelson, Georgia, proposed a mandate for more practical reasons. Nelson has just one police officer, and he is only on duty during the day. Consequently, the proposed law would require residents (with the exception of the mentally ill, individuals convicted of certain crimes, and those who object based on religious principles) to own and maintain a firearm for self-defense purposes. City council member Duane Cronic says this "tells the potential intruder you'd better think twice." But resident Lamar Kellett complains, "This is big government at its worst. Government mandating what a free individual can and will have in his home."

Quoted in Matt Peckham, "Georgia Town Wants to Make Gun Ownership Mandatory," *Time*, March 8, 2013. http://newsfeed.time.com.

relationship to the preservation or efficiency of a well regulated militia, we cannot say that the Second Amendment guarantees the right to keep and bear such an instrument. Certainly it is not within judicial notice that this weapon is any part of the ordinary military equipment or that its use could contribute to the common defense.[23]

The Court also confirmed that the word *militia* referred not just to individual gun owners but to "a body of citizens enrolled for military discipline."[24] In this way the Supreme Court limited the scope of a key term in the Second Amendment.

Violent Triggers

Violent events continued to trigger the enactment of gun control laws in subsequent years. Among the most significant of these were the assassinations of President John Kennedy, Senator Robert Kennedy, and Martin Luther King Jr. in the 1960s, which led to the passage of the Gun Control Act of 1968. This legislation prohibited certain categories of people, such as those convicted of certain types of crimes and those who have been committed to a mental institution, from obtaining firearms or ammunition. It also required gun manufacturers, dealers, and importers involved in interstate gun commerce to be licensed.

The shooting of prominent singer and songwriter John Lennon in 1980 and the attempted assassination of President Ronald Reagan in 1981, both involving shooters who were mentally ill, also brought calls for stricter gun control laws. Nonetheless, no significant new gun control laws were passed during the Reagan administration, because the president was firmly opposed to them. In fact, in 1986 Reagan signed into law the Firearm Owners Protection Act, which provided protections for gun owners while repealing many aspects of the Gun Control Act of 1968. The act ended the licensing of ammunition dealers and the recording of ammunition sales and banned the registration of gun owners. These changes angered many gun control advocates, but they took some measure of comfort from the fact that Democrats in Congress had managed to tack a controversial amendment onto the bill prior to its passage that prohibited the ownership of fully automatic rifles unless they were already registered before the law went into effect.

A Polarizing Issue

Once Reagan's presidency was over, several tough gun control laws were passed—one of them with Reagan's expressed support. Enacted in 1994, the Brady Handgun Violence Prevention Act (more commonly known as the Brady Act) required federally licensed gun dealers to run background checks on anyone wanting to buy a gun to ensure that the person does not have a history of mental illness or criminal behavior. The catalyst behind its passage was Reagan's press secretary, James Brady, who was seriously injured in the attempt on Reagan's life.

In the same year the Brady Act was enacted, President Bill Clinton also signed a federal assault weapons ban into law that prohibited the manufacture of certain semiautomatic weapons and ammunition magazines for civilian use. Although this law ex-

Ronald Reagan on Gun Control

Former president Ronald Reagan was an icon for gun rights advocates because during his presidency he took a strong stance against gun control. Consequently, anti–gun control groups were furious when a pro–gun control group, the United Network of Rational Americans, ran a television ad in March 2013 that suggested Reagan favored gun control. In fact, after his presidency was over, Reagan did seem to soften his stance. In 1991 he expressed support of background checks, stating that they would have prevented his attempted assassination. (This was incorrect, however, since his would-be assassin was mentally ill but had not been legally pronounced as such.) In addition, in 1994 Reagan signed a letter in support of an assault weapons ban. But one of his children later claimed that Reagan's support of both the ban and background checks was due to the fact that he was developing an illness, Alzheimer's disease, that causes mental difficulties. Others say his mind was not yet compromised when he took these positions. Instead, gun control advocates insist that Reagan had simply evolved on the issue, realizing that stronger measures needed to be taken to combat gun violence.

pired after ten years and was not renewed, it created a new level of polarization between the two political parties on the issue of gun control because shortly after its passage, the Republicans gained control of Congress for the first time in forty years. Because they had vigorously campaigned against the ban—while a majority of House and Senate Democrats had endorsed it—the Republicans attributed their political success to their stance against gun laws. Consequently, from this point on, the Republican Party was more outspoken than ever in its opposition to new gun control laws and in its belief that such laws do not reduce gun violence.

It is perhaps not surprising, then, that Republican president George W. Bush was opposed to gun control, although he did support keeping guns out of the hands of criminals and the mentally ill. He believed that there was no need for new gun laws, only a need to work harder to enforce the laws already on the books. However, he also argued that the best way to reduce gun violence was to change aspects of the American culture that encourage gun violence. "Strict enforcement of tough laws is important," he said. "But ultimately, the safety of our children depends on more than laws. It depends on the values we teach them and the kind of culture we create and condone."[25]

"Ultimately, the safety of our children depends on more than laws. It depends on the values we teach them and the kind of culture we create and condone."[25]

— George W. Bush, the forty-third president of the United States.

Even though he is no longer in office, Bush continues to have influence over gun control laws because during his administration, he was able to appoint two anti–gun control justices to the US Supreme Court. In 2008 the court struck down a handgun ban in Washington, DC, that had been enacted in 1976, ruling that the Second Amendment applied to individuals and safeguarded the right to own a gun for the purposes of self-defense within the home. Writing for the majority in the decision, Justice Antonin Scalia said, "We are aware of the problem of handgun violence in this country. But the enshrinement of constitutional rights necessarily takes certain policy choices off the table."[26]

In commenting on this ruling, Democratic senator Dianne Feinstein, a leading gun control advocate in Congress, said, "I believe the people of this great country will be less safe because of it."[27] But Wayne LaPierre, executive vice president of the NRA, said, "I consider this [ruling] the opening salvo in a step-by-step process of providing relief for law-abiding Americans everywhere that have been deprived of this freedom"[28] to own guns. LaPierre is among those who advocate the abolishment of any law that restricts Americans' access to guns, whereas Feinstein is representative of those who are convinced that more gun control laws will mean less gun violence. The debate between these two sides continues today.

Facts

- The gun that killed US president John Kennedy cost only $12.78.

- Reports from the Justice Department indicate that as of June 2013, the background check system in the United States applies to only 60 percent of gun sales because it excludes online sales, purchases at gun shows, and private transactions.

- According to the Brady Campaign to Prevent Gun Violence, in the years since the Brady Act was passed, at least 2 million people have been blocked from purchasing a gun, roughly half of them felons.

- In 1975 the NRA established the Institute for Legislative Action, which lobbies against gun control laws.

- The NRA has approximately 4 million members.

What Role Does Mental Illness Play in Gun Violence?

On July 20, 2012, at a movie theater in Aurora, Colorado, a crowded midnight showing of the Batman film *The Dark Knight Rises* was disrupted by a man who entered through an emergency exit door. Dressed in protective military gear that included a gas mask and a ballistic helmet, he set off tear-gas grenades and began firing at audience members. People screamed and ran as the gunman continued to shoot.

One witness, Jennifer Seeger, later reported, "He pointed the gun at me. I was terrified, so I just dove into the aisle. At that point he started shooting people behind me. . . . I crawled on the ground and I just laid in a ball and waited for him to go up the stairs." Finally, she decided it was time to make her escape. "At that point, I was trying to crawl out but then everybody was crawling back in and saying, 'Don't go over there. He's going to shoot everybody trying to get out of the main doors,' and he was. All I hear is gunshot after gunshot. Just women and children are screaming."[29]

As people rushed from the building, police officers were waiting to help them. They had arrived

> "All I hear is gunshot after gunshot. Just women and children are screaming."[29]
>
> — Jennifer Seeger, survivor of the Colorado theater shooting.

Sheltering in Place

On April 15, 2013, two bombs exploded near the finish line of the Boston Marathon while the event was still in progress. Three people were killed and 264 injured, and in the aftermath people were told to shelter in place. That is, they were supposed to stay in their homes while law enforcement officials hunted for the bombers and tried to determine whether more attacks were imminent. As part of this lockdown, authorities shut down public transportation and closed businesses and schools. Two weeks later, NRA executive vice president Wayne LaPierre suggested that many of those stuck in their homes must have wished they had a gun to defend themselves. He added, "Imagine living in a large metropolitan area where lawful firearms ownership is heavily regulated and discouraged. Imagine waking up to a phone call from the police, warning that a terrorist event is occurring outside and ordering you to stay inside your home." LaPierre's remarks brought a firestorm of criticism, as people accused him of exploiting a tragedy for political gain. But his supporters argue that he was right to emphasize the need for personal protection during a terrorist attack.

Quoted in Alana Horowitz, "Wayne LaPierre: 'How Many Bostonians Wished They Had a Gun Two Weeks Ago?,'" *Huffington Post*, May 4, 2013. www.huffingtonpost.com.

on the scene within just ninety seconds of receiving an emergency call about the shooting. It took longer for ambulances to arrive, though, so some of the officers rushed seriously wounded victims to the hospital in their police cars. Other officers went to help the wounded left inside, where they found a shotgun and some gun magazines on the floor near the victims. The shooter had escaped through the emergency exit door, and at 12:45 a.m. police found him behind the theater near his car and arrested him without resistance. He had shot or otherwise wounded seventy people in his attack; ten of those shot died in the theater and two at the hospital.

The Aurora Shooter

Police identified the shooter as twenty-five-year-old James Eagan Holmes, a graduate student in neuroscience at the University of Colorado–Denver. At the time of the shooting, he was in the process of officially withdrawing from the university. He was also no longer attending classes, in large part because he failed an oral exam in June 2012.

By this time, Holmes was exhibiting signs of a mental illness. He sought help for this illness at the university's student mental health services facility, where he spoke with at least three mental health professionals. One of them, psychiatrist Lynne Felton, reported to campus police that Holmes had made homicidal statements indicating he was a threat to the public. The university did nothing about this report, which was made roughly a month before the shootings.

Meanwhile, Holmes stockpiled weapons. Since he had never been arrested for a crime or determined by a court of law to be mentally ill, it was easy for him to buy guns legally. According to an investigation by the Bureau of Alcohol, Tobacco, Firearms and Explosives, Holmes started buying weapons on May 10, 2012, beginning with the online purchase of tear-gas grenades. He went on to buy two pistols, a semiautomatic rifle, a shotgun, nearly sixty-three hundred rounds of ammunition, bomb-making material, handcuffs, and the components of his ballistic protection clothing and gear. Some of his supplies were purchased online, but the guns were all bought in Colorado gun stores.

Police also determined that Holmes had originally entered the theater in a normal way; he bought a ticket while wearing ordinary clothing and watched about twenty minutes of the movie before leaving through the emergency exit door. He then went to his car, changed into his protective clothing and gear, got some weapons, and returned to the theater through the same exit door. When police arrested Holmes, they found more weapons in his car, and he warned them that his apartment was booby trapped

Residents of Aurora, Colorado, light candles at a vigil across from the movie theater where a shooter killed twelve people and wounded dozens of others in 2012. Questions arose about the shooter's mental health and about the possible influence of violent video images.

with explosives. This indeed proved to be the case. After disarming the bombs, investigators also found prescription medicines for anxiety and depression, as well as paper shooting targets, a Batman mask, and a large amount of alcohol.

Were Violent Images to Blame?

In the aftermath of the attack, people wondered what could have made the killer commit such a horrible act. Many initially placed the blame on the movie that was playing at the time of the shooting. *The Dark Knight Rises* features excessive violence, as does its predecessor in the Batman movie series, and it shows many innocent people being killed. Could these images have somehow inspired Holmes to engage in a mass shooting?

Some studies into this issue suggest that there might indeed be a connection between viewing violent images and committing violent acts. Such studies show that young people who have been exposed to violent media content, especially via violent video games, are somewhat more aggressive afterward. However, theories differ regarding why this aggression might exist. Some researchers argue that where violent video games are concerned, this uptick in aggression is caused by the frustration experienced by players who were not given enough time to become familiar with the game.

Christopher J. Ferguson, associate professor of psychology and criminal justice at Texas A&M International University, noted this problem while conducting a three-year study of the effect of violent video games on children ages ten to fourteen. The results of this study led him to conclude that there is no link between violent content and aggression. He explains that since violent video games

> tend to be more difficult to learn and have more complex controls than non-violent games, it appears that many participants in these experiments may simply have been frustrated by being cut off so quickly before they even learned how to play, rather than by the violent content of the game. Letting them play long enough to learn the game, or simply providing violent and non-violent games of equal complexity, erases the effects.[30]

Others, however, believe that the aggression associated with violent content is not the by-product of emotions associated with the circumstances of a study but instead is a direct result of the violent images being viewed. For example, a committee of the International Society for Research on Aggression examined the results of several studies and concluded that media violence triggers the release of aggressive thoughts or feelings that already exist within the individual. In reporting on this conclusion, Iowa State University says:

> In their report, the commission wrote that aside from being sources of imitation, violent images—such as scenes in movies, games or pictures in comic books—act as triggers for activating aggressive thoughts and feelings already stored in memory. If these aggressive thoughts and feelings are activated over and over again because of repeated expo-

sure to media violence, they become chronically accessible, and thus more likely to influence behavior.[31]

The commission also concluded that repeatedly viewing violent images can make a person view the world differently. Their report stated that in addition to being quicker to access violent thoughts and feelings, "one may also become more vigilant for hostility and aggression in the world, and therefore, begin to feel some ambiguous actions by others (such as being bumped in a crowded room) are deliberate acts of provocation."[32]

The belief that repeated exposure to violent images can alter someone's worldview is also held by communications theorist George Gerbner, who says that violent movies make many people more prone to commit violent acts because of something he calls the Mean World Syndrome. This syndrome occurs when individuals who watch violent content develop misperceptions regarding just how violent the world is. Communications expert David Ropeik explains the Mean World Syndrome by saying:

> Gerbner's idea holds that if we think the world is a "mean" and violent and unsafe place, the kind of world we see again and again in both the news and so much entertainment media, we live our lives accordingly. We buy guns to protect ourselves. . . . We live in gated communities. We support candidates who promise to keep us safe. . . . In a violent and threatening world we are readier to fear "others."[33]

This type of fear, the Mean World Syndrome theory suggests, makes it easier to view others as valid targets of gun violence.

Desensitization

Research has also shown that exposure to violence can desensitize people to it, and some psychologists argue that when people are less disturbed by violence, it is easier for them to commit murder. One of the leading proponents of this idea is Dave Grossman, a former psychology teacher at the US Military Academy at West Point. Grossman argues that playing violent video games hardens players' emotions to the point where they can kill in real life, and he believes that video games condition young people to engage in violent acts by rewarding them during game play for every violent act they commit. He says, "By sitting and mindlessly killing countless thousands of fellow members of your own species without any ramification or repercussions, we are teaching skills and concepts and values that transfer immediately anytime they get a real weapon in their hand."[34]

Other experts argue that the problem is that the media glorifies violence. For example, Steven Paquin, writing for the online news platform PolicyMic, argues that many movies "help cultivate a culture of violence" by showing heroes that "break every rule, regulation, and sense of moral decency to get the bad guy" and do not face any serious consequences for their actions. Such scenarios, he says, send a powerful message to impressionable viewers: "Violence is beautiful, masculine, empowering, and emancipating. Fear, anxiety, distrust, confusion, weakness, anger, hatred, justice, and the greater good are all acceptable reasons for aggression. Thievery, murder, torture, and kidnapping are tolerable, if the person is a 'hero' or 'authority.'"[35] Paquin adds that given how many times movie viewers come across this message, he is not surprised that there are school shootings.

Others, however, argue that it is wrong to blame the media for such shootings, particularly since there are many other aspects of a shooter's life to take into account. For example, forensic psychiatrist Michael Stone says, "I don't think it's the case where a young person sees a violent movie and then from that reason alone, in the absence of another trigger, goes out and decides it's a cool thing to do and buys a gun and shoots a bunch of people. I think it's about some event in his personal life, unrelated to any movie."[36]

In Holmes's case, for example, he was feeling frustrated and angry over his inability to pass a test and continue to pursue his doctorate in neuroscience. Since this meant he would never become famous as a scientist, he might also have had a desire to

"I don't think it's the case where a young person sees a violent movie and then from that reason alone, in the absence of another trigger, goes out and decides it's a cool thing to do and buys a gun and shoots a bunch of people. I think it's about some event in his personal life, unrelated to any movie."[36]

— Forensic psychiatrist Michael Stone.

At a 2013 pro-gun rally in Massachusetts a protester expresses the view that the cause of gun violence is not guns, but mental illness and mental instability. Those who hold this view oppose further restrictions on gun ownership.

obtain notoriety in some other way. As Stone noted about Holmes shortly after the shooting, "He moves himself up from a pathetic nothing to a very important person who's getting his 15 minutes of fame by not only the mass murder, but by dressing up as a cartoon character. That would tend to nail his image even more solidly in the minds of the public who follow the event."[37]

Was Mental Illness to Blame?

In commenting on the way that Holmes was dressed during the shooting, Stone is referring to the fact that Holmes had dyed his hair red to approximate the look of a villain in the Batman movie, the Joker. Holmes apparently identified with this character strongly, since when he was arrested, he said, "I am the Joker."[38] Such an identification, some psychologists say, is a sign that the person has a delusion, which means the individual has a mental illness that can cause him or her to act like the object of his or her identification. For example, University of Toronto psychologist Jonathan Freedman says, "If you have 100 million people watching violent movies and one of them or five of them or 10 of them have a delusion that they are the people in the movie" then these deluded people might "go out and do the same thing as those characters."[39]

As more has become known about Holmes's illness, more people have decided that mental illness was to blame for his actions. Psychiatrist Keith Ablow is one such person. In an editorial titled "It Always Comes Down to Mental Illness," he argues that the shooting in Aurora and similar ones elsewhere are all the result of a failed American mental health system. In fact, Ablow says "the seeds of these tragedies were being sown"[40] when doctors began dispensing pills after seeing patients for only a few minutes and various politicians and government officials started shutting down state hospitals and defunding community mental health centers. He states, "After years of America destroying its mental health care system, leaving it in ruins, as a national disgrace, cases of undiagnosed and untreated mental illness are to blame for the horrific episodes of violence that have made headlines and wrongly fueled gun control legislation."[41]

Ablow wants the effort to reduce gun violence to concentrate on improving the country's mental health system. He argues that in cases of such violence, it is not the weapon that is the problem but the mind of the person wielding the weapon. To support his position, he points to an attack on April 9, 2013, at a college in Houston, Texas, where a mentally ill student stabbed fourteen of his classmates throughout the health sciences building. Ablow says this "should settle the gun control/violence debate, once and for all" because the attacker's weapon was a knife rather than a gun, and even if guns were banned, "there will still be cars, and poisons, and hammers, and axes that can be used to inflict horrible injuries."[42]

"After years of America destroying its mental health care system, leaving it in ruins, as a national disgrace, cases of undiagnosed and untreated mental illness are to blame for the horrific episodes of violence that have made headlines and wrongly fueled gun control legislation."[41]

— Psychiatrist Keith Ablow.

Ending Access to Guns

Nonetheless, most of the mentally ill who commit mass murder do choose to use guns. Therefore gun control advocates argue that at the very least it should be illegal for people who have a serious mental illness to own a gun. As an editorial by Colorado Community Media states, "The vast majority of mentally ill people do not commit crimes, and may actually be more prone to being victimized, experts say. But some individuals with certain types of mental illness are driven to hurt people. And they should not have legal access to guns."[43]

Laws already address this issue by requiring background checks prior to gun purchase that are meant to reveal whether the in-

Delusions and Schizophrenia

Many mass shooters have been males under age thirty-five suffering from either violent delusions or schizophrenia. According to various studies on schizophrenia, the average age for men to develop this illness is 22, but the common age for being admitted into treatment for it is 28, which means there is a six-year gap between onset and treatment. This is because schizophrenia often does not come to the attention of medical professionals until the sufferer has had a psychotic episode, whereby the person exhibits personality changes and has trouble determining what is real and what is not. With delusions, the situation is even more problematic. Here too the sufferer has trouble determining reality, but unless this condition is associated with schizophrenia there is no psychotic episode to bring the person to the attention of professionals. Therefore some experts recommend that colleges mandate yearly mental health checkups for students and provide anonymous hotlines for students to report classmates who are behaving oddly.

tended buyer has been legally diagnosed as mentally ill. However, these background checks often rely on scant information because of poor reporting by the courts. Some state legislators are trying to remedy this problem. In May 2013, for example, a law went into effect in South Carolina that ensures that the names of state residents declared mentally ill by any South Carolina court are entered into a federal database that provides information to gun shop owners conducting background checks.

Another law enacted in California in May 2013 goes a step further. It provides funds and resources for a program that takes handguns and assault weapons away from California residents who bought these weapons legally but have subsequently been declared mentally ill by the courts or have been convicted of a crime. The funding for this program comes from money drawn from fees that people pay when they buy guns in the state. In speaking of this law, Evan Westrup, a spokesperson for California's governor, says, "This bipartisan bill makes our communities safer by giving law enforcement the resources they need to get guns out of the hands of potentially dangerous individuals."[44]

Not in the Database

However, people who have serious mental illnesses do not always come to the attention of the courts and therefore do not exist in any database of the mentally ill. Holmes was one such individual, even though he did exhibit unusual behavior prior to the Aurora shootings. In addition to uttering the remarks that concerned psychiatrist Lynne Felton, Holmes behaved so strangely that other people thought him mentally disturbed. For example, the owner of a gun range said that Holmes left him a voice mail asking about the facility, but "it was this very guttural, very heavy bass, deep voice that was rambling incoherently."[45]

A similar case was that of Jared Lee Loughner, who in January 2011 killed six people and injured fourteen in Tucson, Arizona, while shooting at Representative Gabrielle Giffords (who was shot in the head but survived). Loughner was suspended from his community college in 2010 because he exhibited disturbing behavior and had been caught carrying a knife. One of his classmates wrote in an e-mail to friends in June 2010 that Loughner was a "mentally unstable person . . . that scares the living crap out of me. He is one of those whose picture you see on the news, after he has come into class with an automatic weapon." Political activist and gun control opponent Kayleigh McEnany cites this case, the Holmes case, and several others as proof that "more rigorous mental health monitoring could have stopped these crazed shooters; stricter gun laws would not have."[46] However, in many states the law provides people with the right to privacy when it comes to their mental health records unless their health-care provider has determined that they pose a serious and imminent physical threat to themselves or others, and this limits the kind of reporting that can be done.

Increasing the Database

Some laws have attempted to broaden this definition, so that the threat is not necessarily imminent. For example, in March 2013 New York enacted a law that would require mental health professionals to report to the state any patients that they believe *might* be capable of harming others, so that the state can revoke the gun license of such people and seize their guns. Many of the state's psychologists have spoken out against this requirement. For example, James Knoll, director of forensic psychiatry at New York's Upstate Medical University, complains, "We're being transformed into agents of the state and agents of government control."[47] Others argue that the law criminalizes mental illness, while correctly noting that the mentally ill are statistically no more likely to commit a violent crime than the rest of the population. Surveys have also suggested that the law might make mental health patients less likely to be open about their feelings for fear that they might say something that will get them reported to the government. This fear is compounded by the fact that the law does not require mental health professionals to get a patient's consent or even notify the patient before making a report.

Such encroachments on personal rights give many people pause, especially since mental health experts cannot agree on whether being more aggressive in addressing mental illnesses will solve the

problem of mass shootings. Given this uncertainty, psychologist Georgann Witte argues that instead of focusing on mental illness as a way to solve the problem of mass shootings, people should simply eliminate the weapons that enable mass shootings. She says, "The problem is not that some of our fellow citizens suffer from mental illness, but that powerful weapons and vast quantities of ammunition are potentially accessible to anyone—an undiagnosed and untreated schizophrenic, a murderously jealous spouse, an intoxicated depressive—far beyond our ability to screen, diagnose or treat."[48] In other words, there are many reasons that a person decides to go on a killing spree, and when guns are readily available, it is easier to commit murder (and to commit other crimes as well). Yet it is also true that given the number of guns available in America, it would be difficult to eliminate all access to them. Therefore many experts agree that continued research into the psychological and social causes of gun violence is vital.

Protesters express their support for new gun control laws during a demonstration in New York City in 2012. Several states have enacted stricter laws in connection with the mental health status of potential gun buyers.

Facts

- According to the American Psychiatric Association, only 4 to 5 percent of violent crimes are committed by people with mental illness.

- The American Psychiatric Association reports that one-quarter of all Americans have a mental disorder in any given year.

- Federal crime statistics show that while video game sales more than doubled between 1994 and 2010, the number of young people committing violent crimes dropped by more than half.

- According to the Harvard Injury Control Research Center, a driver with a gun in the car is 77 percent more likely to drive aggressively.

- According to the National Institute of Mental Health, drug and alcohol abuse is far more likely to lead to violent behavior than mental illness.

- According to the National Shooting Sports Foundation, approximately 70 percent of ammunition is for non-hunting use, particularly target practice.

Should Assault Weapons Be Banned?

On the morning of September 6, 2011, thirty-two-year-old Eduardo Sencion left the Carson City, Nevada, house where he lived with family members and drove to the parking lot of a local shopping center. He parked his minivan across three spaces—attracting the attention of at least one person who nearly confronted him about it—and stayed there for several minutes before driving out of the lot. Approximately thirty minutes later he was again spotted in the lot, parked in a different area. He then drove away, and at 8:56 a.m. he entered a neighboring lot belonging to an International House of Pancakes (IHOP) restaurant.

Reports of what happened next vary. The owner of a nearby barbecue restaurant, Ralph Swagler, says that Sencion stepped out of his minivan and immediately shot a woman standing near a motorcycle; Swagler then grabbed a weapon of his own but backed off after realizing that his handgun was no match for Sencion's assault rifle. Swagler says, "I wish I had shot at him when he was going in the IHOP. But when he came at me, when somebody is pointing an automatic weapon at you—you can't believe the firepower, the kind of rounds coming out of that weapon."[49]

Other witnesses, however, say that the woman by the motorcycle was shot after Sencion exited the IHOP after killing people inside. Sencion had gone into the busy restaurant, walked to a back table where five National Guardsmen sat, and shot at them before shooting at others. Still others say that the first person shot in the restaurant was not a guardsman but a woman in her late sixties eating breakfast with her husband. (She was killed; her husband was shot as well but survived.)

In any case, Sencion fired off thirty rounds inside the IHOP before firing off more rounds outside. Some witnesses said he fired at people in the parking lot, others that he spun in a circle while continuing to fire in whatever direction he was pointing. Several businesses were hit, including Swagler's restaurant. Then Sencion shot himself in the head; he later died at a hospital. Investigators

Straw Buyers

Both opponents and proponents of gun control agree that as long as guns continue to be manufactured, criminals will still be able to acquire them. No bans or restrictions, they say, will prevent a determined criminal—who obviously has no compulsion to follow laws—from obtaining weapons. One way criminals do this is by using what police call a straw buyer, someone who legally obtains a gun only to give it to a criminal. One example of a straw buyer is twenty-two-year-old Stevie Marie Vigil of Colorado, who legally bought a gun from a licensed gun dealer in a Denver suburb. Vigil then passed that gun along to a felon, twenty-eight-year-old Evan Ebal, who would not have been allowed to purchase a gun after a background check was run. Ebel then used the gun to kill Colorado Department of Corrections director Tom Clements and pizza delivery driver Nathan Leon. (Evidence later surfaced to indicate that Ebal had shown up at Clements's door posing as the pizza deliveryman.) Ebal was subsequently shot and killed by law enforcement officers after a high-speed chase and shootout, and Vigil was arrested for providing a felon with a gun.

subsequently learned that he was on medication for a mental illness at the time of the attack.

Excluding Sencion, four people were killed in the IHOP attack, three of them guardsmen, and seven people were seriously injured. However, the carnage could have been worse because Sencion had brought far more ammunition with him than he used. He fired 60 to 79 rounds of ammunition but had brought 595 rounds and 20 magazines loaded with 30 rounds each to the scene, along with two assault rifles and a semiautomatic handgun.

More Speed, More Victims

Authorities estimate that the IHOP shooting lasted just eighty-five seconds. Sencion was able to fire so many rounds in such a short time because of the kind of weapon he used, a semiautomatic rifle that had been illegally converted into an automatic rifle. A semiautomatic rifle fires one round, or piece of ammunition (including the projectile known as a bullet), each time the trigger is pressed, whereas an automatic rifle fires rounds continuously as long as the trigger is depressed. In either case these guns can have another round at the ready almost immediately after the previous round is fired. Consequently, both deliver bullets much more quickly than rifles or handguns that are neither fully nor partially automatic. This shared trait has led most people to refer to both semiautomatic and automatic rifles as assault rifles, even though until recently the term *assault rifle* referred only to a fully automatic rifle.

Because both kinds of assault rifles go through bullets rapidly, they typically use high-capacity magazines that hold many rounds. A magazine is an ammunition storage container that is sometimes permanently part of the gun but is much more often capable of being removed and replaced quickly. The most common are twenty- and thirty-round magazines, although James Eagan Holmes, the shooter in the Aurora, Colorado, theater massacre, tried to use a one-hundred-round drum magazine that jammed.

With so much ammunition available to a shooter, assault rifles can kill a large number of people in a relatively short amount of time. They can also create so much chaos that it is difficult for people to try to escape the scene or defend themselves. This was the

The AR-15 assault rifle and 30-round magazine (pictured) have been the subject of heated debate between those who believe such weapons should be banned and those who do not. A person with an assault weapon and high-capacity magazine can shoot many people in a very brief span of time.

case in the IHOP shooting. One witness, Kevin Carrick, who was inside the restaurant at the time of the attack, reports that when the shooting started, "all of a sudden, all hell broke loose. I was eating my food, and the place started shaking. . . . I thought the building was coming apart. Then I turned to my left and saw this big sheet of glass explode. I yelled . . . 'Get down, get down, get down.'" Carrick adds the chaos made it difficult to think. "There were gunshots exploding all around," he says. "You were disorientated because of the concussion, the echo and the sound bouncing off the concrete wall." Some people were therefore slow to react. Carrick says, "I was under the table and saw some people across the way that didn't know what to do. There was a woman standing up, running in circles because she was disorientated, like the rest of us. A kid was standing up, too. They didn't know what to do."[50]

"Close to a War"

Sheriff Mike Haley, the chief law enforcement officer of the county in which the IHOP shooting occurred, reports that what happened inside the restaurant "was as close to a war as most people will ever come, and they were helpless to defend against it." Therefore, Haley says, "I don't see any logic to having assault weapons available to the public."[51]

A National Guardsman wounded in the IHOP attack, Sergeant Caitlin Kelley, agrees. She says, "I can't imagine why we are even selling assault weapons to civilians. There's no reason for an AK-47 or an M-16 or an M-4 [all types of assault rifles] to be in a civilian's home."[52] Similarly, Nevada state assembly member William Horne says, "I'm a gun owner. I believe in people's rights. But I don't know anybody who uses an AK-47 to hunt. To what degree do you need a machine gun to protect your home? Do you need a bazooka?"[53] Many people share this view.

Nonetheless, machine guns—fully automatic rifles—are legal to own in Nevada as long as they are registered with the federal government and the purchaser has undergone a background check. Semiautomatic rifles, however, do not require a background check or any sort of registration or gun license. The IHOP shooting brought calls in Nevada for a ban on the sale of assault rifles in the state. However, Carolyn Herbertson, a lobbyist for the NRA, countered, "I don't believe any more gun laws would have prevented the IHOP shooting."[54] Moreover, she argues that no law should be changed simply as a response to a tragic event, suggesting that bad decisions might be made in the heat of the moment.

"I can't imagine why we are even selling assault weapons to civilians. There's no reason for an AK-47 or an M-16 or an M-4 [all types of assault rifles] to be in a civilian's home."[52]

— Sergeant Caitlin Kelley, survivor of the IHOP shooting.

A Popular Weapon

Opponents of a ban on assault rifles offer several arguments for why enacting such a ban would be a mistake. One of the most common is that a ban would be pointless because assault weapons are not responsible for most of the shooting deaths in America. As Stephen Halbrook, a Virginia lawyer who has represented the NRA, says of assault rifles, "They get a lot of coverage when there's a tragedy with one, but the number of people unlawfully killed with them is small."[55] Indeed, according to the FBI Uniform Crime Reports, out of the 8,583 firearm-related homicides in 2011, 6,220 were committed by handguns but only 323 by rifles—and not all of these were assault rifles.

The United States does not keep records of how many guns are sold each year, only of how many applications there are to buy guns each year. (In 2012, according to the National Instant Criminal Background Check System, there were well over 16 million such applications.) However, in compiling manufacturing figures on a type of assault rifle known as the AR-15 as part of a lawsuit, Halbrook estimated that from January 1986 through June 2012, at least 3.3 million AR-15s were manufactured in the United States but not exported to other countries. Moreover, according to licensed gun dealers, in 2012 the AR-15 was the most popular gun in America.

In many parts of the United States, this rifle is also popular among gang members, who use it both to commit crimes and to defend themselves against members of rival gangs. In Miami, Florida, for example, Police Chief John Timoney says that AR-15s are "the weapon of choice among gangs here. . . . The guns keep coming in, their prices are dropping."[56] Consequently, whereas assault weapons were used in about 4 percent of all Miami homicides in 2004, as of the end of 2012 that number was about 21 percent.

Gang members are typically drawn to two types of assault rifles, the AK-47 and the AR-15. The AK-47 is manufactured in Russia specifically for use in warfare, although the United States allows its import for sporting purposes only. The AR-15 is a civilian version of the US military's standard-issue assault rifle, the M16. In either case, says Detroit police chief Ralph Godbee, "we're talking about weapons that are made for war." He reports that with the AK-47 and AR-15, "you can shoot 50 to 60 rounds within a minute. Within a minute you can literally shoot through brick, shoot through steel."[57] He is concerned about this capability because his city is among those where gang members' attraction to assault rifles is making police work more dangerous. Experts in gun violence note that such guns are increasingly used to kill police officers, whose protective vests typically do not hold up against fire from an assault rifle.

Self-Defense

Largely because assault rifles are popular with criminals, these weapons are also becoming popular with citizens wanting them for self-defense. In fact, in a February 2013 editorial in *American Thinker* magazine, gun rights advocate Mark Almonte says that "assault rifles are the pre-eminent self-defense weapon." In explaining why, he says:

> Assault rifles look and sound intimidating. When you fire a 9mm handgun, it makes a popping noise. When you

Participants in a 2013 protest in Connecticut call on Walmart to stop selling assault weapons. Those who support a ban on assault weapons say such weapons belong only on a wartime battlefield, not in cities and towns across America.

fire an AK-47, it sounds like thunder. Most assault rifles were designed to be effective up to 400 meters. Most handguns are accurate only up to about twenty-five yards. Rifle rounds have twice the velocity and four times the muzzle energy of handgun rounds. Their accuracy and power make assault rifles very effective against multiple attackers.[58]

As an example of a case in which assault rifles were vital for self-defense, Almonte cites the 1992 Los Angeles riots that resulted in businesses being destroyed and people being attacked randomly on the street. As the violence raged around them, a group of Korean shopkeepers gathered on the rooftop of a building and successfully scared away rioters by using shotguns and assault rifles to fire shots into the air. Therefore, Almonte says, "When there's no law and order—only chaos—that's when civilians need assault weapons."[59]

Almonte argues that assault weapons are just as important to the country's defense. He says, "Assault rifles can mean the difference between life and death, between liberty and tyranny. In the hands of law-abiding citizens, assault rifles are a symbol of self-reliance. It's an American value that has defined this country and made it great." He believes that assault weapons are necessary to ensure that dictators will not take over America, because "having an assault rifle tells a despot that the cost to take your freedom will . . . be high."[60]

> "Assault rifles look and sound intimidating. When you fire a 9mm handgun, it makes a popping noise. When you fire an AK-47, it sounds like thunder."[58]
>
> — Mark Almonte, writing in an editorial in *American Thinker*.

Banning Magazines

Assault weapons also seem to be the weapon of choice for people who perpetrate mass shootings. James Eagan Holmes used an AR-15 during the Aurora, Colorado, theater shooting, as have many other mass shooters, sometimes in concert with semiautomatic handguns. Experts in gun violence say that such individuals are typically drawn to assault weapons for two reasons. First, they are more lethal than other guns, and second, they are associated with the military, which appeals to those who want to emulate military-

A Loophole in California's Assault Weapons Law

California's assault weapons ban has not stopped gun manufacturers from selling assault weapons in that state. There is a loophole in the law that makes such sales possible simply by making a minor change in the weapon's design. Specifically, in describing the semiautomatic rifles that fall under the ban, the law states that they are capable of using a detachable ammunition magazine, along with certain other military-style features. But the definition of *detachable* is that no tool is required to remove the magazine from the weapon—and a tool can be anything but the shooter's hand. Consequently, gun manufacturers started putting a button on the rifles that would release the magazine when pressed by the tip of a bullet. In writing about this design change, the Violence Policy Center says, "With the tip of the bullet replacing the use of a finger in activating the release, the button can be pushed and the detachable ammunition magazine removed and replaced in seconds. Compared to the release process for a standard detachable ammunition magazine it is a distinction without a difference." The center says that this "bullet button" has become "the gateway to the California market" for manufacturers of assault rifles.

Violence Policy Center, "Bullet Buttons," May 2012. www.vpc.org.

style attacks depicted in video games or movies. Tom Diaz of the Violence Policy Center says, "The people we're talking about, once they get into 'I want to kill a lot of people,' it's not a leap for them to see that these guns are made and designed for war. And if you look at the industry advertising, that is a consistent theme."[61]

Gang members fighting one another on the streets of American cities also prefer high-capacity magazines. According to one

Chicago high school student who spoke to a reporter for the Public Radio International show *This American Life*, the reason he prefers a thirty-round magazine is obvious: "They got the most shots. You can shoot forever. Let out 15. Run back to where you going. Somebody else come out and let out five more. There you go."[62]

To reduce the number of victims of such weapons, some people argue that the shooter should be forced to reload more often. This, some say, will give potential victims more time to get away and give others time to stop the shooter in the middle of an attack. To support their argument, proponents of limiting the size of magazines note that during Jared Lee Loughner's 2011 attack on Gabrielle Giffords and her constituents in Tucson, Arizona, a woman was able to take away his thirty-round magazine after he stopped shooting to reload it. Consequently, Daniel Vice, a lawyer with the Brady Center to Prevent Gun Violence, says, "If he had been limited to 10 rounds, lives could have been saved."[63]

Indeed, six states already have bans on high-capacity magazines (ones that hold thirty rounds or more): California, Hawaii, Maryland, Massachusetts, New Jersey, and New York. After both the Giffords shooting in Arizona and the IHOP shooting in Nevada, legislators in both states proposed similar bans. Those in favor of a ban argued that getting rid of high-capacity magazines would not harm anyone who wanted to use an assault rifle for a lawful purpose. For example, Carson City sheriff Ken Furlong says, "If you're truly a sport shooter, a 30-round magazine is not relevant. Typically, a 10-round magazine is sufficient. The only purpose is to put a lot of bullets out there."[64] However, Nevada senator Mike McGinness counters, "If [people] have malice in mind, they're going to do it whether they have to change magazines four times or two."[65]

Others argue that the size of the magazine does not matter because it is so easy to exchange one magazine for another. For example, gun rights advocate Jack Lee, who has a degree in criminology, says, "Magazine capacity matters little, as switching magazines only takes a few seconds." In fact, he notes that it can take

"If you're truly a sport shooter, a 30-round magazine is not relevant. Typically, a 10-round magazine is sufficient. The only purpose is to put a lot of bullets out there."[64]

— Carson City sheriff Ken Furlong.

"less than half a second."[66] Lee also argues that an assault weapons ban will fail to reduce violent crime, because the federal ban on assault weapons and high-capacity magazines that passed in 1994 but expired in 2004 failed to do so. As proof, he points to the fact that fourteen mass shootings still occurred during the years of that ban, including one at Columbine High School in Littleton, Colorado, in 1999. Lee also notes that like the 1994 ban, a new ban will likely exempt weapons that have already been sold so that officials will not have to confiscate existing guns, and this will mean that determined shooters can still get their hands on assault weapons.

Guns Versus Knives

But supporters of an assault weapons ban say that even if only a few lives can be spared by such a ban, then the effort will have been worthwhile—and they do believe that fewer people will die if a ban is enacted. As Kristen Rand of the Violence Policy Center notes, "The equation is simple. More guns lead to more gun death, but limiting exposure to firearms saves lives."[67] As an example of how lives can be saved when a killer does not have an assault weapon handy, gun control supporters point to an attack at an elementary school in China in December 2012. In this case a mentally ill man attacked more than twenty children, but because he used a knife instead of a gun, all of the children survived the attack.

William Saletan of *Slate* magazine therefore argues that mental illness should not be the primary concern when trying to come up with ways to reduce gun violence. He says:

> Madmen are everywhere. They strike without regard to gun laws, mental health care, or the national rate of churchgoing. . . . But one pattern holds true: The faster the weapon, the higher the body count. It's not politics. It's logistics. If you stick a knife in your first victim, it takes time to move on to your second. You might need two stabs or more to finish off the first kid. By then, the other kids have begun to flee. Soon, the cops will be here. How much time do you have? At some point, it's time to off [kill] yourself. And all you managed to kill were two lousy kids because the only weapon you had was a kitchen knife.[68]

Saletan reiterates that the key factor in the number of deaths is how fast the weapon can take lives. "Speed kills," he stresses. "Madness pulls the trigger, but the rate of fire drives the body count." Therefore he thinks that people on both sides of the gun control issue need to work together to slow down the gunfire. He says:

> I don't think banning guns will make the problem go away. We don't need another all-or-nothing war between pro-gun and anti-gun ideologues. What we need is a frank, precise, constructive conversation about the problem of high-speed weapons. You don't need rapid-fire weapons to hunt or defend your home. Cops don't need them to shoot down bad guys. And while it's true that passing a law against them won't eliminate them, that's not an argument against legislation. It's an argument for going beyond legislation. The community of gun sellers and enthusiasts must act collectively to track and control the technology of mass murder.[69]

Saletan and others who support his approach acknowledge that it will be difficult to get people to cooperate to this degree. Nonetheless, they are hoping that by focusing the discussion on just one type of gun, they will be able to convince gun rights advocates that they are not calling on an infringement of anyone's right to own a firearm, just the right to own a weapon that should only be available to military personnel.

Facts

- According to a survey of gun dealers by the National Shooting Sports Foundation, 49.1 percent of the AR-15-style rifles sold in 2011 were bought for target shooting.

- In surveying gun dealers, the National Shooting Sports Foundation found that hunting accounted for 22.8 percent of sales and personal protection 28.1 percent in 2011.

- *Mother Jones* magazine reports that from 1982 through 2012, there were thirty-one mass-shooting cases that relied on forty-two guns with high-capacity magazines.

- According to *Mother Jones* magazine, from 1982 through 2012, twenty assault weapons were used in fourteen mass-shooting cases.

- The National Shooting Sports Foundation reports that in 2011 US gun, rifle, and ammunition sales to civilians totaled $4.3 billion, and a third of this amount was spent on bullets.

Would Arming More People Make America Safer?

On the morning of December 14, 2012, twenty-year-old Adam Lanza shot his mother in their home in Newtown, Connecticut. The pajama-clad Nancy Lanza was in her own bed when her son fired four shots into her head using a .22-gauge rifle. Roughly five minutes later he showed up at his former grade school, Sandy Hook Elementary, with a Bushmaster AR-15 assault rifle, two semiautomatic handguns, ten thirty-round magazines, and a combat shotgun that he decided to leave in his car. He was dressed in black and wore a mask.

School was in session, but the building's entrance was locked. (The school required visitors to ring a doorbell and show ID before being allowed inside.) Lanza used his rifle to shoot the glass in the door so he could get in. At the time, faculty members were in a meeting. When they heard the gunfire, three of them—principal Dawn Hochsprung, psychologist Mary Sherlach, and teacher Natalie Hammond—went to see what was going on. Their shouts upon encountering Lanza alerted their coworkers to the danger before Lanza killed Hochsprung and Sherlach. Meanwhile, Hammond ran back into the meeting room, shut the door, and pressed against it to keep it shut. Lanza shot her through the door (she survived her wounds), then turned his attention to the school's classrooms.

By this time, students and teachers had heard gunfire and screams over the school's public address system. It is unclear whether this system had been left on prior to the attack or whether one of the teachers in the meeting turned it on after the initial gunfire. In either case this gave teachers some warning that they and their students might be in danger. Special needs teaching assistant Shari Thornberg, who was in a math-science room devoid of students when the shooting began, says, "We heard pop-pop-pop, pop-pop-pop, and I thought, 'That's a weird noise.' I first thought

Children and Guns

Between December 15, 2012, and May 7, 2013, forty children under age twelve were accidentally killed by a gun in the United States. Many of these cases involved one child shooting another. For example, a four-year-old girl in Missouri was accidentally shot in the head after her playmate found a loaded gun left unattended, and a six-year-old New Jersey boy was accidentally shot in the head by a four-year-old playmate. In commenting on the latter case, a neighbor, Debi Coto, said, "I'm sad for the children involved and their families, but I'm angry with whoever owns that gun and allowed a little child to get hold of it. A 4-year-old can't load a gun. I had just been telling my sister how nice it is to see kids playing together and enjoying themselves, and then this happens." But in another case, involving a five-year-old boy in Kentucky who pointed a loaded rifle at his two-year-old sister and fired, the gun had been made for children and bought for their use with adult supervision. But no adults were present when the accident occurred.

Quoted in Bruce Shipkowski, "Toms River Shooting: 6-Year-Old Boy Dies After Accidental Shot by Playmate," *Huffington Post*, April 10, 2013. www.huffingtonpost.com.

it was the janitor taking down risers and setting up tables." Then over the intercom she heard "more shots, screaming, crying and whimpering," followed by the janitor yelling, "Put the gun down! Put the gun down." Thornberg adds that even after she and two coworkers hid in a closet, "We heard everything over the intercom, though it was muffled because our closet door was closed. We just waited in the closet, saying The Lord's Prayer out loud over and over again, and praying for all staff members and the children."[70]

In one first-grade classroom, substitute teacher Lauren Rousseau tried to hide her students in a bathroom at the back of the room. However, this was apparently the first classroom Lanza entered. He quickly shot and killed Rousseau and all of her students but one, a six-year-old girl who played dead among the bodies.

In another first-grade classroom, students were hiding under desks or in a closet when Lanza walked in and started shooting the children under desks. When some of them bolted for the door, he shot at them, too. Most did not survive, and when the teacher tried to put herself between Lanza and some of his targets, he shot and killed her as well. However, at one point his gun either jammed or needed to be reloaded, and in these moments a few children managed to escape. The children in the closet were spared as well, apparently because Lanza did not realize they were there.

Two teacher's aides were also shot and killed while trying to shield children. Other adults hid children in various places in the school or barricaded their doorways to keep their young charges safe. Meanwhile, a school secretary called 911. Authorities now estimate that within fifteen minutes of this call being made, Lanza used one of his handguns to shoot himself in the head. They believe that the shooter committed suicide because he realized police were on the scene. Nonetheless, since the police did not know for quite some time afterward that Lanza was dead and that no other shooters were on the scene, officers had to move into the school slowly and evacuate the classrooms carefully, one by one.

Even More Weapons

Lanza killed twenty-six people at the school, twenty of them children, all of the children between six and seven years old. Investigators

later determined that he had fired 154 shots from his assault rifle in less than five minutes and that he had carried enough ammunition with him to have been able to kill all 450 children enrolled at the school if he had had more time. Witnesses said that Lanza did not speak while shooting, and investigators also determined that he reloaded often, sometimes without even waiting for all of the rounds within a magazine to be used up. In addition, he shot every one of his victims more than once; one six-year-old boy was shot eleven times. As a result, the murder scene was so horrific that police told young survivors to close their eyes as they led them out of the school.

After the massacre, investigators went to Lanza's home and found still more weapons, including two rifles, over a half dozen knives, three samurai swords, and sixteen hundred rounds of ammunition. (At the time, Connecticut law allowed a twenty-year-old like Lanza to own rifles, shotguns, and other long guns; however, he was too young to own or carry any kind of handgun.)

Angel figures in a wooded area near Sandy Hook Elementary School in Newtown, Connecticut, offer a remembrance of the children killed in a mass shooting at the school in 2012. The shooting reignited America's emotionally charged gun control debate.

They also found a check from his mother inside a holiday card telling him the money was for another firearm, a certificate showing that Lanza was a member of the NRA, information on other mass shootings, and some disturbingly violent photographs. They were unable to access his computer to see whether there were disturbing writings as well, because Lanza had intentionally damaged it before embarking on his killing spree.

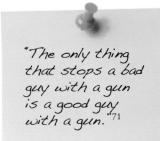

"The only thing that stops a bad guy with a gun is a good guy with a gun."[71]

— NRA vice president Wayne LaPierre.

However, investigators did determine that Lanza's mother was worried about her son's mental health and might have been planning to have him committed to a mental health facility. A family friend also reported that Lanza, who had poor social skills, was bullied while attending Sandy Hook Elementary School and that this is why his mother transferred him to a different school. In addition, Lanza was known to spend hours playing the first-person shooter video game *Call of Duty*, which featured military combat scenarios, and had fought with his mother over his desire to join the military. Nonetheless, she had supported his interest in guns and often took him to a shooting range.

All of these pieces of information fueled arguments over whether Lanza's mother, a mental illness, poor social skills, a violent video game, bullying, or the prevalence of guns in the home were to blame for the shooting. In addition to all of the typical arguments about what might have caused this terrible tragedy, some people began to suggest that if staff members at the elementary school had been armed, they could have stopped the attack before lives were lost.

Arming School Personnel

Almost immediately after the Newtown shooting, the NRA promoted the idea that teachers should be armed. "The only thing that stops a bad guy with a gun is a good guy with a gun," said NRA vice president Wayne LaPierre at a press conference roughly a week after the shooting. He stated that the NRA was calling for the immediate passage of a federal law that would "appropriate whatever is necessary, to put armed police officers in every school in the nation."[71] He then promoted an NRA-backed program that would train retired police and military personnel to serve as volunteer school security officers. This was necessary, he said, because another Adam Lanza could already be planning a similar attack.

Many pro-gun lawmakers immediately agreed with LaPierre that schools needed armed personnel. Some also said that keeping guns out of schools increased the likelihood that children would be shot. In arguing this point, Tennessee state senator Frank Niceley said, "Look at it this way, you never see one of these whacko shooters go to a gun show and start shooting. They don't go down to the police station and start shooting. They go to places we advertise are gun-free."[72] In other words, Niceley believes that just the perception that a public place is vulnerable can trigger an attack.

He and other Republican politicians in at least six states crafted laws that, if passed, would make it possible for existing school personnel to be armed. By placing the responsibility for defending the school on existing school personnel rather than on armed guards, lawmakers felt that schools could be made safer more quickly and at much less cost to taxpayers. However, there was some disagreement about which school employees should be armed. Texas representative Louie Gohmert suggested that it should be the principal. He said of Sandy Hook principal Hochsprung, "I wish to God she had had an M-4 in her office, locked up so when she heard gunfire, she pulls it out . . . and takes him out and takes his head off before he can kill those precious kids."[73]

> "Look at it this way, you never see one of these whacko shooters go to a gun show and start shooting. They don't go down to the police station and start shooting. They go to places we advertise are gun-free."[72]
>
> — Tennessee state senator Frank Niceley.

However, some believed that the responsibility should instead rest with someone that a killer would not recognize as a symbol of authority and therefore might not guess would be armed.

One person commonly suggested for this role is the school janitor. In fact, in January 2013 city officials in Montpelier, Ohio, proposed a program that would arm every janitor in their school district, and four janitors volunteered to take part in a two-day training course funded by the district. Some of Montpelier's parents thought this was a good idea. Teresa Hickman, a mother of three in the district, which had roughly one thousand students in grades K–12, said, "I don't have a problem with it. With all the shootings going on in these little schools this will make me feel more at peace."[74] But Shannon Siler, a mother of two, felt uneasy about janitors carrying guns. She said, "I am a little leery. I know they are going to be doing all this training and stuff, but what if a janitor goes psychotic?"[75]

In South Dakota parents and legislators had similar concerns about a law proposed in their state that would allow school employees with a permit to carry a concealed weapon to bring their guns to work. Democratic state senator Angie Buhl said, "I'm not sure a janitor is necessarily qualified to take down an armed shooter."[76] But others argue that extensive training could make a janitor or other school personnel qualified to defend a school.

However, Niceley proposed that this training be conducted in secret. He explained that if a killer walked into a school, "if he doesn't know which teacher has training, then he wouldn't know which one had [a gun]." Niceley also suggested that if the killer was confronted by bullets coming from an unexpected source, this would end the crisis more quickly because "these guys are obviously cowards anyway and if someone starts shooting back, they're going to take cover, maybe go ahead and commit suicide like most of them have."[77] For similar reasons, Oklahoma state senator Ralph Shortey suggested that not just one person but many should be armed, and not just inside schools but at any school event. He said, "Allowing teachers and administrators with concealed-carry permits the ability to have weapons at school events would provide both a measure of security for students and a deterrent against attackers."[78]

> "I'm not sure a janitor is necessarily qualified to take down an armed shooter."[76]
>
> — South Dakota state senator Angie Buhl.

Crisis Situations

Many law enforcement experts, however, disagree with the idea of arming not just school personnel but others in the general population. In large part this is because such experts doubt that ordinary citizens would be able to handle the psychological pressures associ-

SAVE OUR
CHILDREN

ARM OUR
SCHOOLS

ated with mass shootings and similar incidents. As the police chief of Medford, Oregon, Tim George, notes, "In crisis situations there are a lot of very complex things happening all at once and you have to constantly train for deadly force incidents."[79] One of the biggest concerns with introducing additional guns into such settings is that in their eagerness to stop a bad guy, someone might accidentally kill innocent bystanders caught in the crossfire. As an example, Dean Michener of the New Hampshire School Boards Association says, "The chances an armed teacher will hit a child are high."[80]

Many also say that having more guns in the general population would result in more deaths, not less, after individuals found themselves incapable of confronting someone determined to kill as many people as possible. It is difficult to respond quickly enough to a crisis situation, police say, and not everyone can go through with the decision to kill someone. As Randy Davis, a retired Kansas police officer, says, "The people that would have guns—they're not trained to be a police officer that knows how to attack a situ-

At a pro-gun rally in Louisiana in 2013 a protester calls for the arming of teachers in the nation's schools. The National Rifle Association, among others, has urged such action based on the view that potential shooters will be less likely to attack schools if personnel are armed.

ation. If you are putting a life-and-death piece of equipment into your hands, are you prepared to take the next step?"[81]

Bill Bond, the principal of a school in Paducah, Kentucky, where a fourteen-year-old gunman shot students at a school prayer group in 1997, knows all too well the difficulty of responding to such a situation. Bond says that he would not have been able to act quickly enough because the shooter "stood against a wall and shot eight kids and three of them died. That took 12 seconds. It is fast."[82] Bond also doubts that he would have been able to shoot the attacker had he been carrying a gun himself. In fact, he says that had he approached the young man with a drawn weapon—instead of with a calming tone, which helped him convince the killer to give up—he, too, would have been shot. "I was able to take the gun from him," he says, "but I believe if I had been armed, I would have been dead."[83]

Bond's story also counters the argument that without access to a weapon, a person confronting a shooter will inevitably end up getting shot. This is the implication of South Dakota state representative Betty Olson when she says of the potential victims of such shooters, "They're going to be dead regardless, the way I see it, so [being armed] is the only chance they've got."[84] But as Bond discovered, there is always the possibility that a shooter can be talked out of taking lives.

New Laws to Arm Citizens

Nonetheless, several states have moved ahead with laws allowing citizens to arm themselves. Just four months after the Newtown shooting, South Dakota passed legislation that allows school personnel to carry guns in the schools. Arkansas legislators passed a law that allows college teachers who already have permits to carry concealed guns to bring them to work. Still another state, Kansas, passed a law allowing its public schools, universities, and colleges to arm employees of their choosing. However, schools can decide not to designate anyone as a gun carrier, and teachers cannot be forced to carry a gun against their will.

Other states with similar laws in the works abandoned them in the face of opposition from teachers, administrators, and parents. This was the case in Oklahoma, for example, where state representative Steve Martin says, "As a rule, it's very difficult to find educators and administrators that support the idea of putting arms in the schools, for whatever reason."[85] In Indiana, where a proposed law would have required an armed security officer in every school during school hours, Indiana governor Mike Pence explained his lack of support for the bill by saying, "Decisions that are nearest and dearest to our hearts ought to be made by parents and local school officials."[86]

Another reason often cited for opposition to arming not just school personnel but anyone who spends a lot of time around children is the concern that this would increase the likelihood that a child could accidentally gain access to a weapon and kill

A Maryland teacher, participating in a 2013 demonstration in Washington, DC, publicly expresses her view about having armed teachers in schools. Those who oppose the arming of school personnel say the danger to students would be greater in schools filled with guns.

a classmate or playmate, either intentionally or unintentionally. As Kansas parent Judith Deedy of Mission Hills says sarcastically, "Guns in schools with curious children. What more could possibly go wrong there?"[87] Others, however, say that adequate safety measures will keep guns from children, and that their children will be safer overall if there is a gun available to protect them from attack.

Opinions on whether or not ordinary citizens should be armed are often dependent upon political party. Polls have consistently shown that far more Republicans than Democrats favor arming the populace. For example, in an April 2–3, 2013, poll by the *Huffington Post*, 62 percent of Republicans favored arming teachers and other school officials, whereas only 15 percent of Democrats did. Independents were slightly more likely to support the idea of arming teachers and administrators (44 percent were in favor, 32 percent opposed), and men were slightly more likely than women to support the idea (45 percent to 31 percent). This is not to say, however, that a majority of Republicans want concealed weapon permits to be handed out without some restrictions. Only 14 percent of all respondents in the poll said that gun laws should be less strict, 30 percent felt they should remain the same, and 49 percent felt that gun laws should be tougher.

Arming Everyone

Members of the Armed Citizen Project, however, believe that the majority of people who are neither criminals nor mentally ill should be armed. Based in Houston, Texas, this nonprofit group is working to give guns and gun training to people in mid- to high-crime neighborhoods. As of May 2013 the group had plans to give shotguns away for free in fifteen US cities by the end of the year, including Chicago, New York, and Tucson. Each recipient of a gun must submit to a background check and be trained by group members on how to use the gun. In addition, each shotgun comes with a trigger-locking device to give the recipient control over who can fire the gun.

In explaining the reason for the project, the group's website states, "Gun-control advocates often argue that an increase in guns in an area will lead to an increase in crime, while gun-rights advocates often believe that fewer guns result in more crime. Both sides believe that their policies will result in less crime, and it is about time that our side begins to act with the conviction and courage that it will take to win the debate." The site says that to prove that more guns will reduce crime, the pro-gun activists must "actively encourage the increased presence of defensive weapons in society."[88]

There are as yet no undisputed statistics regarding whether more guns do reduce crime. But some people say that regardless of whether this is the case, they would not want to live in an America that can only be safe if most adults are walking around with concealed weapons. Kansas state senator Tom Hawk holds this view. "My personal hope in my life . . . is that we might promote a

Vigilantism

Some experts say that increasing the number of guns in America will also increase vigilantism, and one of the most prominent examples of a vigilante is George Zimmerman. This twenty-eight-year-old Hispanic man encountered a seventeen-year-old black teenager, later identified as Trayvon Martin, walking through his neighborhood late one night in February 2012 and immediately became suspicious of him. The captain of his neighborhood watch, Zimmerman had made forty-six calls to police since 2006 to report similar concerns. This time he told the dispatcher that he thought the young man was "up to no good" and had something in his hand, implying that Martin might be carrying a weapon. The dispatcher told Zimmerman to leave the suspect alone and said police were on the way. Nonetheless, an armed Zimmerman confronted Martin, and few minutes later Martin was dead. Accounts of how he was shot are in dispute, but investigators say that instead of a weapon, the young man had been carrying only an iced tea and a bag of Skittles.

safer and less violent world," he explains. "And for me, having an expansion of weapons, even for good reasons, does not get to the kind of world that I want to live in."[89] But others counter that it is better to have a well-armed citizenry than to live in fear of being left unprotected during a mass shooting.

Facts

- Within four months of the Newtown shooting, four states—Colorado, Connecticut, Maryland, and New York—passed stricter gun control measures.

- In the aftermath of the Newtown shooting, state legislators across the United States introduced more than fifteen hundred gun-related bills, with legal experts determining that roughly half of them would weaken gun control laws.

- According to the Children's Defense Fund, in 2007 more preschool-aged children were killed by guns than police officers were killed in the line of duty.

- The Centers for Disease Control and Prevention reports that homicide is the third leading cause of death among children and young adults and the leading cause of death among African American youth.

- The Centers for Disease Control and Prevention says that less than 2 percent of youth homicides occur at school, even though children spend more than a third of their waking hours there.

- An April 2013 poll by the *Huffington Post* found that 39 percent of parents with children under age eighteen in the household said that schools would be made more safe by allowing teachers to carry guns, while 35 percent said they would be made less safe.

Are There Alternatives to Traditional Gun Control Measures?

I n March 2013 Jonathan Stimpson, an eighth grader in Darien, Connecticut, won a gold medal in the national Scholastic Art & Writing Awards contest because of his essay "Gun Control: A Call to Action." In this essay he complained that the polarization of America's political parties on the issue was leading to an inability to make meaningful changes that would keep people safe from gun violence. "Gun control in the United States is one of the most complex and divisive issues we face. Any mention of it results in a fiery battle of ideological beliefs," he wrote, adding that "simply 'taking a side' or taking 'the liberal or conservative' point of view will only prolong the pathetic divisiveness that plagues any attempt at solving this very real issue."[90]

Stimpson also complained about the fact that the politicians and the media typically spend a lot of time talking about mass shootings while ignoring the other types of gun violence that plague America. He said, "Mass shootings aren't the only manifestation of lax gun control; cities such as Chicago, Detroit, New York, New Orleans, and Memphis have dozens of gun murders each year. These all but go unnoticed by the media, but in reality we all have to face the grim truth that families have to grieve, every day from gun violence. Only when politicians decide to lead, and people advocate, will [the mass shooting in] Newtown [Connecticut] serve as the end of an era."[91]

Stimpson called on the country's leaders to come up with new ideas related to solving America's gun violence problem. To start the discussion of innovative approaches, he called attention to the

Smart Guns

In January 2013 President Barack Obama ordered a report on advances in gun safety technology and encouraged gun manufacturers to produce smart guns. Also called personalized guns, smart guns are weapons that have some kind of advanced technology that allows them to recognize authorized users. For example, a gun might have a fingerprint or grip recognition feature, or as is the case with one gun well into development, it might require the user to enter a numeric code into a wristwatch that then transmits the code to the gun via radio waves. But whatever the personalization feature, the gun will not work for someone other than the authorized user. Supporters of such weapons say this will reduce gun violence because such weapons would be useless if taken, for example, by a criminal, a mentally ill person, or a young person. But gun owners oppose them on the grounds that they might stop working at inopportune moments, will probably be too expensive, and have already inspired legislators to suggest laws mandating that once smart guns are available for purchase, they will be the only kind of gun that can legally be sold.

idea that guns be treated like automobiles, which are also objects capable of killing people. Stimpson argues that cars and guns are similar because "both have their uses, but when used irresponsibly have the potential to compromise public safety." Therefore, he says:

> Guns should not be treated like a God given right, but rather a privilege that is acquired only by doing the necessary steps. Among the "necessary steps" used to regulate cars that should be transposed for guns include: strict licensing, renewal of licenses, and entry into a central database, which if combined will help assure better enforcement and reduced ease of accessibility.[92]

Stimpson also proposed requiring every citizen to have gun insurance, which would be similar to car insurance.

Gun Insurance

Among the first to suggest mandating gun liability insurance was John Wasik of *Forbes* magazine. In the aftermath of the Newtown, Connecticut, shooting in December 2012, he argued that because of the Second Amendment, there was no way that guns were ever going to completely go away. Therefore, he said, people needed to start focusing on what is possible.

"What we can do is to look at gun sales through the lens of social economics," he explained. He then called for the establishment of "market-based risk pricing," saying, "Let's agree that guns as weapons are inherently dangerous to society and owners should bear the risk and true social costs."[93] This would mean that both owners and sellers of guns would be required to purchase liability insurance according to relative risk, whereby people who are more at risk for directly or indirectly causing gun violence would pay more for their insurance than people unlikely to cause this violence.

Wasik expanded on this explanation in an April 2013 *Forbes* article, after his idea had attracted a great deal of attention. He said, "Ideally, high-risk households would have to pay more and take more safety measures, so at-risk people wouldn't have easy access to them. Responsible buyers would pay lower premiums for taking gun-safety classes, using gun locks and safes."[94] These premiums would be used to cover the costs associated with gun violence, giving relief to people injured in shootings and to the families of victims.

In response to this idea, legislators in California, Massachusetts, Connecticut, and Maryland have proposed mandating gun insurance in their states. In addition, in April 2013 Representative Carolyn Maloney put forth a bill titled the Firearm Risk Protection Act, which if passed into law would mandate that all gun owners carry liability insurance. This law would also impose a fine of $10,000 on any seller who does not confirm that the buyer of a weapon is covered by firearm insurance and on any buyer who has managed to acquire a weapon without purchasing such insurance.

Others have proposed providing either an alternative to such a mandate or a supplement to it, whereby gun owners and sellers would pay a tax on their guns that would provide additional monies to victims of gun violence. David Hillshafer argues in *Skeptic* magazine that an approach requiring both insurance and tax payments would help in capturing criminals because "people at very high risk to commit gun violence would be unlikely to receive affordable liability insurance. Criminals and those who are irresponsible will likely have uninsured and untaxed firearms, and tax evasion is a crime. This would give law enforcement another method to throw criminals in jail for possessing guns illegally."[95]

Ammunition Restrictions

Another economics-based approach to the problem of gun violence is the proposal to tax ammunition, which Wasik lauds because it puts the cost of gun violence on those who cause it and might result in a reduction of such violence. He explains, "There's a long history of taxing things that are dangerous: Alcohol and tobacco are on top of the list. It's a long-held economic principle that taxing harmful activities can reduce their occurrence."[96] Putting a higher cost on ammunition might also cut down on gang warfare and other attacks that involve a lot of gunfire because, proponents of this approach say, gang members will be less likely to spray bullets wantonly into a crowd of rivals if bullets are expensive.

Most Americans, regardless of their views on gun control, can agree with the sentiment expressed by a young man taking part in a 2013 demonstration in New York City. Some efforts are underway to find new ways of dealing with this problem.

In addition to or instead of taxation, people who believe bullets should be targeted for control have suggested laws that would limit access to ammunition. Federal law already prohibits anyone under age eighteen from buying ammunition for a rifle and under age twenty-one for a handgun. However, other regulatory issues are primarily left to the states, and only a few currently control the sale of ammunition even minimally. Illinois and Massachusetts require buyers to show an identification card issued to firearm owners along with another ID in order to purchase ammunition. New Jersey requires ammunition sellers to keep a record of their sales that includes the name and address of the purchasers, who must have a firearm permit. A New York law that will go into effect in January 2014 will require an instant background check for ammunition buyers and also require ammunition sellers to register with the state.

In some cases cities have enacted their own laws to regulate ammunition. For example, in Los Angeles, California, ammunition dealers must keep a record of sales and make them available on demand to police. In the state capital, ammunition buyers are required to provide not only their name and address but a thumbprint so that sellers can make sure they are not in a federal database of criminals. However, a proposed California law that would require buyers statewide to submit to a background check is meeting resistance. The same is true for a federal law proposed in January 2013 by Democratic US senator Richard Blumenthal of Connecticut that would require people to have a background check before every ammunition purchase. There have also been suggestions that ammunition manufacturers be required to put serial numbers on bullets that can be traced to registered users. In addition, some people want guns to be required to leave a uniquely identifiable, traceable mark on each bullet as it exits the gun barrel.

Ammunition Bans

Others have proposed banning certain types of ammunition. For example, California has a statewide ban on selling, using, and possessing "unreasonably dangerous" ammunition, and some of its cities have proposed laws that are more specific. In April 2013 San Francisco proposed one that would ban the possession of hollow-point bullets that expand on impact in a way that causes more harm to the victim than other kinds of bullets. In May 2013 the Los Angeles City Council drafted a law that would make it illegal to own high-capacity ammunition magazines, after previously banning the sale and transfer of such magazines.

More extreme are proposals that America follow Switzerland's model of ammunition limits, whereby people can only possess ammunition in certain places. Many Swiss people own guns—the country has 2.3 to 4.5 million guns among a population of less than 8 million people—yet gun violence there is much less frequent than in the United States. (In 2010 there were only about 0.5 gun homicides per 100,000 inhabitants

"Is there any study out there that shows a ban on high-capacity magazines prevent shootings or save lives? I don't think there is . . . in fact, there isn't."[97]

— Colorado state representative Mark Waller.

in Switzerland, whereas in the United States the rate was about 5 per 100,000 people.) Some people attribute this to the fact that Swiss citizens need a permit to buy ammunition, and ammunition bought at a shooting range must be used there or stored there. Other ammunition is supposed to be stored in a central arsenal.

But gun rights advocates generally oppose the creation of laws that would require permits for ammunition or otherwise restrict its sale or leave a record of who bought it and used it. They also argue that there is no proof that regulating ammunition reduces gun violence. For example, in regard to a Colorado law that would ban residents from purchasing ammunition magazines of more than fifteen rounds, state representative Mark Waller says, "Is there any study out there that shows a ban on high-capacity magazines prevent shootings or save lives? I don't think there is . . . in fact, there isn't."[97] Another common argument is that such bans will have no effect on street crime because criminals will always be able to get ammunition. Illinois gun shop owner Mike Hale, in questioning Illinois's need for ammunition restrictions, expresses this view by saying, "As a criminal, a criminal can get anything he really wants. They don't abide by the laws."[98] This is the same argument typically used against laws that propose to restrict access to guns.

> "As a criminal, a criminal can get anything he really wants. They don't abide by the laws."[98]
>
> — Illinois gun shop owner Mike Hale.

A National Database of the Mentally Ill

Many gun rights advocates would prefer to focus instead on identifying and registering the mentally ill. In fact, in response to the Sandy Hook shooting, the NRA proposed creating an "active" national database to register the mentally ill. This would be an aggressive effort that goes beyond the current system and is carefully maintained.

In advocating changes to the current system, Wayne LaPierre of the NRA complains, "We have no national database of these lunatics. . . . 23 states are still putting only a small number of records into the system and a lot of states are putting none. So when they go through the National Instant Check System and they go to try to screen out one of those lunatics, the records are not even in the system."[99] At present, sharing the health records of those who have been adjudicated mentally ill is a state responsibility. Eight states already have their own databases, and an additional thirty states report their mental health records to the National Instant Criminal Background Check System. But even among the thirty states that report at the national level, there are failures in providing the names of those who have serious mental illnesses.

In order to replace this state-based system with a national database, there would have to be a law establishing universal criteria for reporting. Some experts say coming to a consensus on this would be difficult, especially since it is hard enough to get mental health professionals to agree on commitment criteria. Mental health professional Randall W. Bachman reports:

> As someone who was involved with changing the commitment law in another state, I can testify how difficult and contentious making even a common-sense modification of such laws can be. We were trying to amend the statute to allow the courts to take into account past history when considering commitment, not just immediate danger. This process was a classic clash of civil liberties versus public safety.[100]

In other words, the proposed changed would have based the determination of mental illness on past threats as well as present ones, and even this was a matter of controversy.

Subjective Determinations

Nonetheless, the American Academy of Nursing and other organizations have called for dangerous histories rather than simply legal determinations of mental illness to be taken into account in determining who should not own a gun. The academy says, "Lawmakers are urged to empower health care professionals to identify and counsel individuals with high-risk danger behaviors and to restrict gun purchases to individuals with dangerous histories using a national database." The organization adds that laws should be

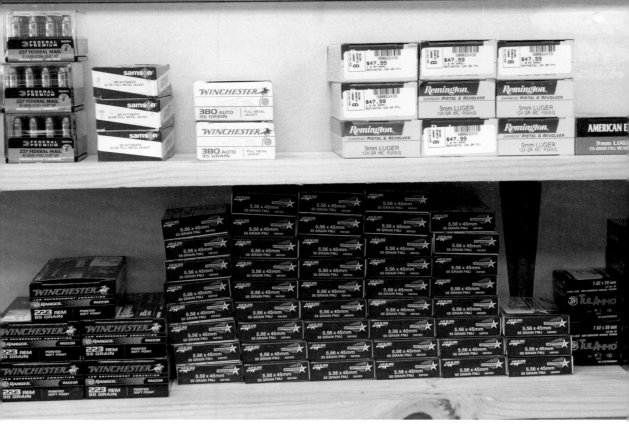

strengthened "so that high-risk individuals, including those with emergency, temporary, or permanent protective or restraining orders or those with convictions for family violence, domestic violence and/or stalking are prohibited from purchasing firearms."[101] However, not all restraining orders are based on behaviors that would warrant taking away someone's right to own a gun, and there have been many cases of one person lying about another person's behavior in an attempt to get a restraining order.

Critics of the academy's position also take issue with the idea that determinations of dangerousness, which rely not only on facts but on opinions, could be made by any health professional as opposed to strictly psychiatrists or psychologists. They say that only experts in mental health are qualified to judge mental health, and they argue that it is vital for such judgments to be made carefully because a label of poor mental health might impact other aspects of that person's life. For example, it might prevent someone from

Among ideas being discussed are laws that target ammunition. Some of these ideas, including tight controls on ammunition sales and storage, are likely to raise many objections among US gun owners.

getting a job or being able to join the military. Critics also worry that someone whose name has been entered into a national database might have difficulty removing it from that list if the individual's mental health status changes.

Universal Background Check

Another criticism of the national database has to do with its fairness. Although the NRA strongly supports the creation of a database for the mentally ill, it just as strongly opposes the establishment of a universal background check system that would result in a registry of all gun owners. This position, many people say, is hypocritical, and they question why America should force the mentally ill but not gun owners to participate in a national registration system.

In commenting on the NRA's opposition to a universal background check for gun owners, an editorial on the news and commentary site *Eclectablog* notes, "So, if you're mentally ill, you need to be on a national registry. . . . But if you buy a gun, putting your name on a registry is putting you 'under the thumb of the federal government.'"[102] Gun control advocates want a universal background check system because they believe it will combat crime. However, gun rights advocates counter that this can already be accomplished through a more aggressive enforcement of existing laws. As Andrew Arulanandam of the NRA explains, "We have adequate laws on the books. If someone is breaking the law, go after them. If not, they should be left alone. That's the NRA position."[103]

But others point out that law enforcement efforts require funding, and there is often not enough money for them. A prominent example of this is the fact that for years Congress has failed to provide adequate funding for the National Instant Criminal Background Check System. In 2011, for instance, the US budget authorized that $375 million be spent, in large part to provide states with incentives to report mental illnesses—yet Congress only appropriated $20 million for this purpose. Similarly, the Justice Department does not have the manpower to

"We have adequate laws on the books. If someone is breaking the law, go after them. If not, they should be left alone. That's the NRA position."[103]

— Andrew Arulanandam of the NRA.

Private Sellers

Whereas legislators have long required gun shops to conduct background checks on prospective gun buyers, sellers at most gun shows are not required to do so, nor are private parties selling guns on the Internet. Therefore, people who know they would not pass a background check often turn to gun shows and the Internet to illegally buy and sell guns. For example, in October 2012, when forty-two-year-old Zina Haughton of Milwaukee, Wisconsin, got a restraining order against her husband because he had threatened her with violence, he became unable to buy a gun legally. But, he was able to find someone on the Internet who would sell him one without conducting a background check. After meeting this seller in a McDonald's restaurant parking lot, Radcliffe Haughton went to his wife's place of employment and killed not only her but two of her coworkers and injured four others before killing himself. As a result of such crimes, federal legislators have proposed new laws that would regulate sales on the Internet of guns and/or ammunition, but gun rights advocates strongly oppose such laws.

prosecute all of the gun purchasers each year who lie while providing information necessary for their background checks or to catch all of the people who legally buy a gun only to hand it over to a criminal who should not have one.

Experts in gun violence also say that more money should be spent on funding efforts to teach people how to store guns safely to prevent them from falling in the wrong hands. After the Newtown, Connecticut shooting, many people noted that the shooter's mother apparently did nothing to prevent her son from killing her with her own gun in her own home prior to going on his rampage at Sandy Hook Elementary School. Consequently, in commenting on how to protect schools from similar massacres, parent Shannon

Siler of Montpelier, Ohio, says, "There is a need to beef up security. . . . But, it all starts at home. Lock your guns up."[104]

However, there is no way to force people to lock up their guns in their own homes. Police cannot enter private property to check on whether legal gun owners are taking proper safety precautions. This would be a violation of their constitutional rights—and such rights are at the heart of many aspects of the gun control controversy. As Randall W. Bachman notes, "We have gun control already in the United States—individuals are prohibited from possessing automatic weapons and sawed-off shotguns, for example. So the issue is not whether we have gun control. The issue is what kind of gun control will effectively reduce the slaughter of the innocents while respecting Second Amendment rights."[105] Bachman calls on people to work together to develop reasonable gun safety laws, but others argue that in order to do this, people must first set aside political ideology. Only by transcending politics, they say, can Americans come up with common-sense solutions to gun violence that will balance the need to protect rights with the need to protect the innocent.

Facts

- According to the National Shooting Sports Foundation, approximately 10 billion rounds of ammunition are sold annually.

- Swiss law enforcement authorities report that only about three hundred gun crimes are committed in Switzerland every year, most of them suicides and crimes of passion.

- A Quinnipiac University poll released in March 2013 found that nine out of ten people backed the concept of making it harder for criminals and people with a mental illness to get a gun.

- A Quinnipiac University poll released in March 2013 found that 48 percent of respondents worried that the government would use reports of newly developed mental illnesses to confiscate guns already bought legally.

- According to the Brady Campaign to Prevent Gun Violence, nine out of ten Americans want universal background checks, including three out of four NRA members.

- As of April 2013 FBI statistics show that just 0.35 percent of all background checks completed by the FBI turned up cases where someone convicted of a crime was trying to buy a firearm legally.

Source Notes

Introduction: Protection or Threat?

1. Quoted in Twitchy, "Colorado Students Testify Against, for Concealed Carry on Campus; Rape Victim Told Statistics 'Not on Her Side,'" March 4, 2013. http://twitchy.com.
2. Quoted in Lynn Bartels and Kurtis Lee, "Colorado Gun Bills: Lawmakers Spar for Seven Rounds of Bills," *Denver Post*, March 4, 2013. www.denverpost.com.
3. Quoted in Investors.com, "Dem State Senator to Rape Victims: No Guns for You!," editorial, March 7, 2013. http://news.investors.com.
4. Quoted in Katie Pavlich, "Colorado Democrat Lectures Rape Survivor Amanda Collins About Rape 'Statistics,'" *Townhall.com*, March 5, 2013. http://townhall.com.
5. Quoted in Ryan Parker, "Colorado Sen. Evie Hudak Responds to Criticism over Comments to Rape Victim," *Denver Post*, March 5, 2013. www.denverpost.com.
6. Quoted in Parker, "Colorado Sen. Evie Hudak Responds to Criticism over Comments to Rape Victim."
7. Quoted in Will C. Holden, "State Sen. Tells Rape Victim Gun Wouldn't Have Prevented Attack, Later Apologies," Fox31 Denver, March 5, 2013. http://kdvr.com.
8. Quoted in Larry Elder, "How Often Are Guns Used in Self-Defense?," *Orange County Register* (Santa Ana, CA), July 30, 2012. www.ocregister.com.
9. Quoted in Investors.com, "Dem State Senator to Rape Victims."
10. Quoted in Katie Pavlich, "Rape Survivor: A Call Box Above My Head While I Was Being Brutally Raped Wouldn't Have Helped," *Townhall.com*, February 20, 2013. http://townhall.com.
11. Quoted in Twitchy, "Rape Survivor Amanda Collins Hits Back at Anti-Gun State Sen. Hudak: 'You Weren't There,'" March 6, 2013. http://twitchy.com.
12. Quoted in Ryan Parker, "Colorado Sen. Evie Hudak's Concealed Carry Stats Don't Apply in Case," *Denver Post*, March 6, 2013. www.denverpost.com.
13. Quoted in Medical News Today, "Suicide Risk, Political Conservatism, and Church Membership," April 9, 2013. www.medicalnewstoday.com.

14. Quoted in Jason Howerton, "Colorado Dem to Rape Survivor: A Gun Wouldn't Have Helped You Against Rapist Because 'Statistics Are Not on Your Side,'" TheBlaze, March 5, 2013. www.theblaze.com.

15. Quoted in Medical News Today, "Suicide Risk, Political Conservatism, and Church Membership."

Chapter One: What Are the Origins of the Gun Control Controversy?

16. Quoted in Michael Buchanan, "Patrick Purdy Kills Five School Children, Wounds 30 Others," *Criminal Law Blog*, DeThomasis & Buchanan, January 16, 2012. www.reasonabledoubt.org.

17. Quoted in Murderpedia, "Patrick Edward Purdy." http://murderpedia.org.

18. Quoted in Murderpedia, "Patrick Edward Purdy."

19. Quoted in *Time*, "Slaughter in a School Yard," editorial, June 21, 2001. www.time.com.

20. US Constitution, Second Amendment.

21. Adam Winkler, "Did the Wild West Have More Gun Control than We Do Today?," *Huffington Post*, September 9, 2011. http://www.huffingtonpost.com.

22. Quoted in Peter Duffy, "100 Years Ago, the Shot That Spurred New York's Gun-Control Law," *City Room* (blog), *New York Times*, January 23, 2011. http://cityroom.blogs.nytimes.com.

23. United States v. Miller, 307 US 174 (1939).

24. United States v. Miller.

25. Quoted in On the Issues, "George W. Bush on Gun Control," April 28, 2013. www.ontheissues.org.

26. Quoted in Adam Liptak, "Justices Refuse Case on Gun Law in New York," *New York Times*, April 15, 2013. www.nytimes.com.

27. Quoted in CBSNews.com, "Supreme Court Shoots Down D.C. Gun Ban," February 11, 2009. www.cbsnews.com.

28. Quoted in CBSNews.com, "Supreme Court Shoots Down D.C. Gun Ban."

Chapter Two: What Role Does Mental Illness Play in Gun Violence?

29. Quoted in CBSNews.com, "Aurora Witnesses Describe Shooter's Entrance, Chaos," July 20, 2012. www.cbsnews.com.

30. Christopher J. Ferguson, "Video Games Don't Make Kids Violent," *Time*, December 7, 2011. http://ideas.time.com.

31. Iowa State University News Service, "Special Commission on Media Violence Confirms Aggression Link, Includes ISU Professor," August 23, 2012. www.news.iastate.edu.

32. Quoted in Iowa State University News Service, "Special Commission on Media Violence Confirms Aggression Link, Includes ISU Professor."

33. David Ropeik, "How Risky Is It, Really?," *Psychology Today*, July 25, 2012. www.psychologytoday.com.

34. Dave Grossman, "The Violent Video Game Plague," *Knowledge of Reality*, no. 17. www.sol.com.au.

35. Steven Paquin, "Are Violent Movies to Blame for Mass Shootings?," PolicyMic, 2013. www.policymic.com.

36. Quoted in Joe Satran, "*Dark Knight* Shooting Renews Question of Violent Movie Impact," *Huffington Post*, July 21, 2012. www.huffingtonpost.com.

37. Quoted in Satran, "*Dark Knight* Shooting Renews Question of Violent Movie Impact."

38. Thomas Peipert and P. Solomon Banda, "James Holmes, Suspected Aurora, Colorado 'Dark Knight Rises' Shooter: 'I Am The Joker,'" ABC Action News, July 20, 2012. www.abcactionnews.com.

39. Quoted in Satran, "*Dark Knight* Shooting Renews Question of Violent Movie Impact."

40. Keith Ablow, "It Always Comes Down to Mental Illness," Fox News, April 10, 2013. www.foxnews.com.

41. Ablow, "It Always Comes Down to Mental Illness."

42. Ablow, "It Always Comes Down to Mental Illness."

43. Colorado Community Media, "Turning the Gun Debate to Mental Illness," OurHighlandRanchNews.com, May 3, 2013. www.ourcoloradonews.com.

44. Quoted in Patrick McGreevy, "Gov. Brown OKs Funds to Confiscate Guns from Criminals, Mentally Ill," *Los Angeles Times*, May 1, 2013. www.latimes.com.

45. Quoted in George Zornick, "Three Ways Sensible Gun Control Could Have Prevented Aurora Shootings," *Nation*, January 9, 2013. www.thenation.com.

46. Kayleigh McEnany, "Guns Don't Kill People, Deranged Men Do," TheBlaze, April 12, 2013. www.theblaze.com.

47. Quoted in James T. Mulder, "Gun Law's Focus on Mentally Ill Stirs Anger and Confusion," *Syracuse.com*, March 16, 2013. www.syracuse.com.

48. Georgann Witte, "Why Mental Health Screening of Gun Buyers Is No Answer," *Hartford (CT) Courant*, January 25, 2013. http://articles.courant.com.

Chapter Three: Should Assault Weapons Be Banned?

49. Quoted in NBCNews.com, "Nevada IHOP Shooter Was 'Gentle, Kind Man,'" September 7, 2011. www.nbcnews.com.

50. Quoted in *RGJ.com*, "Customer in Carson City IHOP Shooting Recounts Attack, Says He Doesn't Feel like a Hero," September 7, 2011. www.rgj.com.

51. Quoted in Martha Bellisle, "Carson City IHOP Rampage Brings Call to Change State Gun Laws," *RGJ.com*, October 24, 2011. www.rgj.com.

52. Quoted in Bellisle, "Carson City IHOP Rampage Brings Call to Change State Gun Laws."

53. Quoted in Bellisle, "Carson City IHOP Rampage Brings Call to Change State Gun Laws."

54. Quoted in Bellisle, "Carson City IHOP Rampage Brings Call to Change State Gun Laws."

55. Quoted in Erica Goode, "Rifle Used in Killings, America's Most Popular, Highlights Regulation Debate," *New York Times*, December 16, 2012. www.nytimes.com.

56. Quoted in Jesse Jackson, "Police Chiefs Are Right: Ban Assault Weapons," *Chicago Sun-Times*, July 31, 2012. www.suntimes.com.

57. Quoted in Jackson, "Police Chiefs Are Right."

58. Mark Almonte, "Why Do Civilians Need Assault Weapons?," *American Thinker*, February 12, 2013. www.americanthinker.com.

59. Almonte, "Why Do Civilians Need Assault Weapons?"

60. Almonte, "Why Do Civilians Need Assault Weapons?"

61. Quoted in Erica Goode, "Rifle Used in Killings, America's Most Popular, Highlights Regulation Debate."

62. Quoted in Mark Follman, Gavin Aronsen, and Jaeah Lee, "More than Half of Mass Shooters Used Assault Weapons and High-Capacity Magazines," *Mother Jones*, February 27, 2013. www.motherjones.com.

63. Quoted in Bellisle, "Carson City IHOP Rampage Brings Call to Change State Gun Laws."

64. Quoted in Bellisle, "Carson City IHOP Rampage Brings Call to Change State Gun Laws."

65. Quoted in Bellisle, "Carson City IHOP Rampage Brings Call to Change State Gun Laws."

66. Jack Lee, "7 Reasons Why an Assault Weapons Ban Will Fail to Reduce Violent Crime," PolicyMic, 2013. www.policymic.com.

67. Quoted in Bellisle, "Carson City IHOP Rampage Brings Call to Change State Gun Laws."

68. William Saletan, "Speed Kills," *Slate*, December 14, 2012. www.slate.com.

69. Saletan, "Speed Kills."

Chapter Four: Would Arming More People Make America Safer?

70. Quoted in Gary Stoller, "School Shooting Survivor Tells Her Story," *USA Today*, December 19, 2012. www.usatoday.com.

71. Quoted in Peter Overby, "NRA: 'Only Thing That Stops a Bad Guy with a Gun Is a Good Guy with a Gun,'" transcript, NPR, December 21, 2012. www.npr.org.

72. Quoted in Evan McMorris-Santoro, "Tennessee Considers Training and Arming Schoolteachers to Protect Against Shootings," TPM, December 18, 2012. http://tpmdc.talkingpointsmemo.com.

73. Quoted in Dave Jamieson, "Louie Gohmert Says More Guns Are Answer to Preventing Mass Killings," *Huffington Post*, December 16, 2012. www.huffingtonpost.com.

74. Quoted in Mark Reiter, "Armed-Janitor Plan Draws Mixed Reaction from Montpelier Parents," TheBlade, January 13, 2013. www.toledoblade.com.

75. Quoted in Reiter, "Armed-Janitor Plan Draws Mixed Reaction from Montpelier Parents."

76. Quoted in *Black Hills Pioneer* (Spearfish, SD), "Conn. Deaths to Spark Gun Debate in SD Legislature," December 18, 2012. www.bhpioneer.com.

77. Quoted in McMorris-Santoro, "Tennessee Considers Training and Arming Schoolteachers to Protect Against Shootings."

78. Quoted in Randy Krehbiel, "Two State Lawmakers Say Teachers Should Be Armed," *Tulsa (OK) World*, December 17, 2012. www.tulsaworld.com.

79. Quoted in Meredith Bennett-Smith, "Oregon State Rep. Dennis Richardson: Teachers with Guns Could Have Stopped Connecticut Shooting," *Huffington Post*, December 17, 2012. www.huffingtonpost.com.

80. Quoted in Associated Press, "Even in Pro-Gun States, Bid to Arm Teachers Stalls," MLive, April 8, 2013. www.mlive.com.

81. Quoted in Brad Cooper, "Kansas Weighs Letting Teachers Carry Guns," *Kansas City (MO) Star*, March 12, 2013. www.kansas.com.

82. Quoted in Matt Sledge, "Arming Teachers, School Cops Could Cause More Harm than Good, Experts Say," *Huffington Post*, December 20, 2012. www.huffingtonpost.com.

83. Quoted in Sledge, "Arming Teachers, School Cops Could Cause More Harm than Good, Experts Say."

84. Quoted in *Black Hills Pioneer* (Spearfish, SD), "Conn. Deaths to Spark Gun Debate in SD Legislature."

85. Quoted in Associated Press, "Even in Pro-Gun States, Bid to Arm Teachers Stalls."

86. Quoted in Associated Press, "Even in Pro-Gun States, Bid to Arm Teachers Stalls."

87. Quoted in Cooper, "Kansas Weighs Letting Teachers Carry Guns."

88. Armed Citizen Project, "Why Is This Fight Important?," 2013. http://armedcitizenproject.org.

89. Quoted in Brent D. Wistrom, "Lawmakers OK Allowing Educators to Carry Guns in Schools, Approve Making Kansas-Made Guns Immune from Federal Laws," *Wichita (KS) Eagle*, April 5, 2013. www.kansas.com.

Chapter Five: Are There Alternatives to Traditional Gun Control Measures?

90. Jonathan Stimpson, "Gun Control: A Call to Action," *Darien (CT) News,* March 29, 2013. www.dariennewsonline.com.

91. Stimpson, "Gun Control."

92. Stimpson, "Gun Control."

93. John Wasik, "Newtown's New Reality: Using Liability Insurance to Reduce Gun Deaths," *Forbes*, December 17, 2012. www.forbes.com.

94. John Wasik, "Gun Insurance: An Economic Argument," *Forbes*, April 3, 2013. www.forbes.com.

95. David Hillshafer, "The Mass Murderer Problem," *Skeptic*, Winter 2013, p. 24.

96. Wasik, "Gun Insurance."

97. Quoted in Kurtis Lee, "High-Capacity Ammo Bill, Passes Voice Vote in Colorado House," *Denver Post*, February 15, 2013. www.denverpost.com.

98. Quoted in Mike Rush, "Illinois One of Few States with Regulations on Internet Ammo Sales," KSDK.com, July 23, 2012. www.ksdk.com.

99. Quoted in *Eclectablog*, "NRA Fights for National Mental Illness Registry After Fighting Against Gun Registry for Years," December 27, 2012. www.eclectablog.com.

100. Randall W. Bachman, "Would a National Mental-Health Registry Have Prevented Sandy Hook?," *MinnPost*, January 10, 2013. www.minnpost.com.

101. American Academy of Nursing, "American Academy of Nursing Supports Assault Weapons Ban," press release, February 6, 2013. www.aannet.org.

102. *Eclectablog*, "NRA Fights for National Mental Illness Registry After Fighting Against Gun Registry for Years."

103. Quoted in Dan Freedman, "Study Finds Mexican Gangs Prefer High-Powered Assault Rifles," *Houston Chronicle*, May 29, 2011. www.chron.com.

104. Quoted in Reiter, "Armed-Janitor Plan Draws Mixed Reaction from Montpelier Parents."

105. Bachman, "Would a National Mental-Health Registry Have Prevented Sandy Hook?"

Related Organizations and Websites

American Psychiatric Association (APA)

1000 Wilson Blvd., Suite 1825
Arlington, VA 22209-3901
phone: (703) 907-7300
website: www.psych.org

Founded in 1844, the APA is the largest psychiatric organization in the world. It represents more than thirty thousand psychiatric physicians, and its mission is to promote high-quality care for people with mental disorders. Its website provides information on a variety of issues related to mental health.

Armed Citizen Project

PO Box 541039
Houston, TX 77254
website: http://armedcitizenproject.org

This organization works toward arming law-abiding citizens in mid- to high-crime cities across the United States. To this end, it provides people with weapons and trains them in their use at no cost.

Brady Campaign to Prevent Gun Violence

1225 Eye St. NW, Suite 1100
Washington, DC 20005
phone: (202) 898-0792
website: www.bradycampaign.org

The Brady Campaign to Prevent Gun Violence supports policies and projects related to gun safety, gun control, and background checks on all gun sales. Its goal is to reduce gun deaths and injuries, and to this end its website offers articles related to gun violence and its prevention.

Bureau of Alcohol, Tobacco, Firearms and Explosives (ATF)

99 New York Ave. NE
Washington, DC 20226
phone: (202) 648-7080
website: www.atf.gov

The ATF is a government agency charged with investigating and enforcing laws related to firearms, explosives, and alcohol and tobacco products. Its law enforcement efforts also encompass cases of arson, bombings, terrorism, and other violent crimes. The agency's website provides information on such cases.

Centers for Disease Control and Prevention (CDC)

1600 Clifton Rd.
Atlanta, GA 30333
phone: (800) 232-4636
website: www.cdc.gov

The CDC works toward improving and protecting the health of Americans. To this end, it conducts research related to health problems, including injuries and deaths related to gun violence. Its website offers information about a variety of issues related to people's health and well-being.

Federal Bureau of Investigation (FBI)

935 Pennsylvania Ave. NW
Washington, DC 20535-0001
phone: (202) 324-3000
website: www.fbi.gov

The FBI is a government agency charged with enforcing the criminal laws of the United States, including those related to gun violence. Its website offers crime-related news as well as information on its efforts to reduce crime.

Harvard Injury Control Research Center

677 Huntington Ave.
Boston, MA 02115
phone: (617) 432-8080
website: www.hsph.harvard.edu/hicrc

Part of the Harvard University School of Public Health, the Harvard Injury Control Research Center supports research, education, training, and other efforts related to injury and violence in America. It also offers webcasts, available through its website, of discussions related to violence and public health, such as a January 2013 panel on gun violence and a December 2012 interview related to the Newtown tragedy.

National Institute of Mental Health (NIMH)

6001 Executive Blvd.
Bethesda, MD 20892
website: www.nimh.nih.gov

Part of the US Department of Health and Human Services, the NIMH supports research into mental illnesses in order to improve the understanding and treatment of such illnesses and to work toward their prevention, recovery, and cure. Its website provides articles about a variety of mental disorders.

National Rifle Association (NRA)

11250 Waples Mill Rd.
Fairfax, VA 22030
phone: (800) 672-3888
website: http://home.nra.org

Formed in 1871, the NRA is both a firearms education organization and a powerful political organization that lobbies against gun control laws and promotes its stance on Second Amendment rights. Its website provides information about NRA activities and prominent individuals within the organization.

National Shooting Sports Foundation

Flintlock Ridge Office Center
11 Mile Hill Rd.
Newtown, CT 06470-2359
phone: (203) 426-1320
www.nssf.org

Formed in 1961, the National Shooting Sports Foundation supports firearm manufacturers, distributors, and retailers as well as shooting ranges and other businesses related to sport shooting. It also works to promote and protect hunting and shooting sports and offers information and courses on gun safety.

US Department of Justice

950 Pennsylvania Ave. NW
Washington, DC 20530-0001
phone: (202) 514-2000
website: www.justice.gov

The US Department of Justice enforces US laws, works to ensure public safety against foreign and domestic threats, and engages in efforts to prevent and control crime and to punish those who break the law. Its website offers news about prominent law enforcement cases.

Violence Policy Center

1730 Rhode Island Ave. NW, Suite 1014
Washington, DC 20036
phone: (202) 822-8200
website: www.vpc.org

The Violence Policy Center works toward reducing deaths and injuries from gun violence. To this end, it supports research, education, and advocacy related to gun safety. Its website offers a variety of gun-related articles and information.

Additional Reading

Books

Matt Doeden, *Gun Control: Preventing Violence or Crushing Constitutional Rights?* Breckenridge, CO: Twenty-First Century, 2011.

Larry Gerber, *The Second Amendment: The Right to Bear Arms.* New York: Rosen Central, 2011.

Louise Gerdes, *Gun Violence.* San Diego, CA: Greenhaven, 2010.

Kenneth McIntosh, *Outlaws and Lawmen: Crime and Punishment in the 1800s.* Broomall, PA: Mason Crest, 2010.

Christine Watkins, *Guns and Crime.* San Diego, CA: Greenhaven, 2012.

Daniel W. Webster and Jon S. Vernick, eds., *Reducing Gun Violence in America: Informing Policy with Evidence and Analysis.* Baltimore, MD: Johns Hopkins University Press, 2013.

Adam Winkler, *Gunfight: The Battle over the Right to Bear Arms in America.* New York: Norton, 2011.

Internet Sources

Citizens Crime Commission of New York City, "Mass Shooting Incidents in America (1984–2012), 2013. www.nycrimecommission.org/initiative1-shootings.php.

Matthew Herper, "Searching for Hard Data on Guns and Violence," *Forbes*, December 16, 2012. www.forbes.com/sites/matthewherper/2012/12/16/searching-for-hard-data-on-guns-and-violence.

Ezra Klein, "Twelve Facts About Guns and Mass Shootings in the United States," *Wonkblog, Washington Post,* December 14, 2012. www.washingtonpost.com/blogs/wonkblog/wp/2012/12/14 /nine-facts-about-guns-and-mass-shootings-in-the-united -states.

Lynn Langton, "Firearms Stolen During Household Burglaries and Other Property Crimes, 2005–2010," US Department of Justice Crime Data Brief, November 2012. http://bjs.gov/con tent/pub/pdf/fshbopc0510.pdf.

Brad Plummer, "Why Are Mass Shootings Becoming More Common?," *Wonkblog, Washington Post,* December 14, 2012. www .washingtonpost.com/blogs/wonkblog/wp/2012/12/14/why -are-mass-shootings-becoming-more-frequent.

Index

semiautomatic rifles, 41
Sencion, Eduardo, 39–41
Sherlach, Mary, 52
Shortey, Ralph, 58
Siler, Shannon, 58, 75–76
Skeptic (magazine), 68
smart guns, 66
Stimpson, Jonathan, 65–67
Stone, Michael, 31
straw buyers, 40
substance abuse, 38
suicide, 8
   as percentage of all gun
      deaths, 10
Sullivan Act (NY, 1911),
      18–19
surveys
   on arming school personnel,
      62, 64
   on defensive gun use, 8
   of gun dealers on reasons for
      gun purchases, 51
   on gun laws, 62
   on gun restrictions for
      criminals/mentally ill, 77
   on universal background
      checks, 77
Swagler, Ralph, 39
Switzerland, annual number of
   gun crimes in, 77

This American Life (radio
   show), 48
Thompson, Adam, 6
Time (magazine), 14
Timoney, John, 44

Uniform Crime Reports
   (Federal Bureau of
   Investigation), 44
United Network of Rational
   Americans, 22
United States v. Miller (1939),
   19–21
universal background checks,
   22, 74–76
   gun sales excluded from, 24
   private gun sales exempted
      from, 75
   support for, 77
   See also National Instant
      Criminal Background
      Check System

Vice, Daniel, 48
video games
   sales of, youth crime rates
      and, 38
   violent, link between
      aggression and, 29–31
Vigil, Stevie Marie, 40
vigilantism, 63
Violence Policy Center, 47

War of 1812, 15
Washington, George, 15
Wasik, John, 67–68
Westrup, Evan, 35
Wilson, James Q., 8
Winkler, Adam, 17
Witte, Georgann, 37

Zimmerman, George, 63

Picture Credits

About the Author

Patricia D. Netzley is the author of more than fifty books for teens and adults. She also teaches writing and knitting and is a member of the Society of Children's Book Writers and Illustrators.